Leaders Make It Happen!

An Administrator's Guide to Data Teams

Leaders Make It Happen!

An Administrator's Guide to Data Teams

BRIAN A. McNULTY

AND

LAURA BESSER

LEAD+
LEARN
PRESS

ENGLEWOOD, COLORADO

The Leadership and Learning Center
317 Inverness Way South, Suite 150
Englewood, Colorado 80112
Phone 1.866.399.6019 | Fax 303.504.9417
www.LeadandLearn.com

Published by Lead+Learn Press, a division of Houghton Mifflin Harcourt.

Library of Congress Cataloging-in-Publication Data

Besser, Laura.
    Leaders make it happen! : an administrator's guide to data teams / Laura Besser and Brian McNulty.
        p. cm.
    Includes bibliographical references and index.
    ISBN 978-1-935588-00-9 (alk. paper)
  1. School management and organization. 2. Teacher-principal relationships. 3. School improvement programs. 4. Educational accountability. I. McNulty, Brian A., 1948- II. Title.
    LB2805.B467 2010
    371.2'07--dc22

                                                                                    2010043816

ISBN 978-1-935588-00-9

Printed in the United States of America

17 16 15 14 13   04 05 06 07 08 09

Contents

Acknowledgments

Together, Laura and Brian would like to thank the following contributors: Doug Reeves, Kristin Anderson, Tony Flach, Cheryl Dunkle, Angela Peery, Barb Pitchford, Juan Cordova, Jay Trujillo, and Jennifer Wildman.

I would like to dedicate this book to my wife, Donna, who has tirelessly supported me through all of my own personal and professional leadership challenges. Without her I would not have been successful in my own work and life. I would also like to recognize my children, Emmett and Mia, who taught me about leadership and humility. Lastly, I would like to recognize Dr. Doug Reeves, upon whose own work I have heavily relied in this book. His research, insights, and actions are a continuing example of what effective leadership is.

—BRIAN A. MCNULTY

I would like to dedicate this book to the three boys in my life: my husband, Mike, and our two beautiful sons, Vincent and Nicholas, for their patience, love, and support. I'd also like to thank Katie Schellhorn for being such a champion for this work and providing guidance throughout the development of the book. I'd like to thank my Dad and Mom for being such wonderful models in my life and for their continuous encouragement and support.

—LAURA BESSER

Recognition

The improvement framework presented in this book would not exist were it not for the involvement and commitment of 48 urban, suburban, and rural school districts across the state of Ohio. Their dedication and hard work over the last three years in the development, implementation, and ongoing evaluation of this work cannot be overstated. The direct leadership of the Quad Leads along with design team members and Great Lakes East Comprehensive Center (Learning Point Associates) staff members must also be recognized. The expansion of this work to over 300 districts statewide would not have been possible without the support of both the regional Educational Service Centers (ESCs) and School Support Team (SST) members.

The Buckeye Association of School Administrators (BASA), and especially Jerry Klenke, Kirk Hamilton, Kathleen Lowery, Patricia Brenneman, and Rosemary Tolliver, also need to be recognized for their commitment to and involvement in this work, especially in the development of the Ohio Leadership Development Framework that served as a foundation for this work. (See www.ohioleadership.org)

Most of all, however, the Ohio Department of Education (ODE) should be recognized for its leadership and commitment to this work. State Superintendent Deborah S. Delisle, Associate Superintendent Cynthia Lemmerman, and the Director of the Office for Exceptional Children, Kathe Shelby should be noted for their personal commitment to this work. Two key individuals at the Ohio Department of Education, Dr. Stephen Barr and Dr. Debora Telfer, need to be personally recognized for leading in this work. Their knowledge, insights, understanding, and vision brought this work from research into practice across the state. It has been an honor and the professional experience of a lifetime to work with them on this critical systemic work.

About the Authors

Brian A. McNulty, Ph.D., is the Vice President of Leadership Development for The Leadership and Learning Center.

Brian brings 30 years of experience as a nationally recognized educator in leadership development to his current position at The Leadership and Learning Center. Prior to this, he served as the Vice President for Field Services at Mid-continent Research for Education and Learning (McREL). Before coming to McREL, he was an Assistant Superintendent for Adams County School District 14 and the Assistant Commissioner of Education for the Colorado Department of Education.

Brian's work and writing have been featured in books, scholarly journals, and periodicals throughout the world. An author of more than 40 publications, Brian's last book, *School Leadership that Works: From Research to Results*, was a best-selling ASCD publication and was coauthored with Robert Marzano and Tim Waters.

In addition to being a leading authority on leadership development, Brian's extensive experience in working with schools and districts, his knowledge of the research on school and district effectiveness, and his ability to translate this research into practical applications have created the opportunities for him to work as a long-term partner with school districts, state education agencies, and other educational service agencies.

Laura Besser is a Professional Development Associate and Director of Content with The Leadership and Learning Center.

Laura is an instructional leader who combines powerful research and best practices in her approach to helping educators. She works with educators at all levels to improve instructional and leadership practices. Laura provides professional development support, and her expertise in standards, assessment, data analysis, instruction, and leadership results in high-quality professional learning.

Laura was a pioneer in the Data Teams process, and as a building principal she saw dramatic gains in teaching and learning as a result of using the Data Teams model. Her experience as a leader in the process will help any school or district wanting to use Data Teams. Laura's expertise in the Data Teams process will help all leaders use the practices of monitoring and feedback to sustain the process and get results.

Laura has helped to create and revise many of the seminars and services that The Leadership and Learning Center provides. Laura contributed to the Lead + Learn Press publication *Data Teams: The Big Picture.*

Data Meets Collaboration

From Professional Learning Communities (PLCs) to Data Teams

Data Teams are the single best way to help educators and administrators move from "drowning in data" to using information to make better instructional decisions. What makes the Data Teams process distinctive is that we are not just looking at student scores, but at the combination of student results, teaching strategies, and leadership support. The essential question is, "What can we do tomorrow to help students and teachers achieve their goals?" Data Teams give professionals respect, reinforcement, and feedback—the keys for improved impact on student learning.

DOUGLAS REEVES, 2009

The Leadership and Learning Center's Data Teams "roots" began in 2000, but the idea of structured collaboration is not a new concept to most professional organizations; in fact, Tom Peters refers to professional collaboration as an essential building block of any organization (2003). Data Teams are designed for structured collaboration with learning as a central goal. The learning that occurs in these settings is not isolated to students; teachers, principals, and district leaders are actively involved in professional learning that refines their leadership and instructional practices. Covey (2004) says that "people who have made a commitment to continual learning, growth, and improvement are those who have the ability to change, adapt, and flex with the changing realities of life, and become fundamentally equipped to produce in any area of life." Data Teams are the strongest forms of professional development and are structured to get results in teaching, learning, and leadership.

As educational leaders, we create the conditions for structured, professional collaboration to occur. We do so by bringing Data Teams to the teacher or classroom level, to the building level, and to the central office. The Data Teams process combines the best of both worlds: structured collaboration and effective use of data. Therefore, it is a process that can be used by teachers, students, principals, administrators, central office personnel, and classified support educators. As the Data Teams structure is used at different levels, the data-driven process does not change; however, it is shaped to meet the needs of the different types of teams and different types of data. Despite the different looks of a Data Team, the purpose remains central: Data Teams exist to improve teaching and leadership and, as a result, to improve student learning and accelerate achievement levels for all students.

In this book, we will provide research, rationale, and strategies for Data Teams implementation in your system. We will also introduce three different types of Data Teams: district, building, and instructional. In the third section of the book, we will emphasize the important components of a Data Teams framework and provide specific steps to aid the successful implementation of Data Teams.

USING COLLABORATION AND DATA AS A FRAMEWORK

Why should schools use data? While this may seem like an obvious question, Chapter 1 will provide an overview of the sense of urgency to combine the practices of collaboration and use of data to focus school improvement efforts. Schmoker (2006) paraphrases Jim Collins when he says that it's time to confront the "brutal facts" and that we can no longer afford to operate in a complacent manner. He goes on to say that we need to expose teaching and leadership practices that are contributing—or sadly, in some cases, not contributing—to increased learning for all students. As Schmoker says, it's time to turn school improvement "on its head." We can do so by using a structure that combines the use of data and collaboration to improve results.

DATA TEAMS

In Section Two we will look at the different types of Data Teams: District Data Teams (DDTs), Building Data Teams (BDTs), and Instructional Data Teams (IDTs). Each team uses the same processes; however, the look and feel of each team will be unique to the different levels.

Data Teams at the District Level

District Data Teams (DDTs) exist to improve instructional practice. The team includes the superintendent, a school board member, central office staff, the principal, a teacher or teachers, and stakeholders that include parents and business and community leaders. The team leads improvement work driven by the review of data collected at the district level. Teams engage in a data-driven decision-making dialogue that includes using data, analyzing data, developing focused goals and strategies, conducting deep implementation, and providing a monitoring and feedback cycle. District Data Teams also bring alignment for the whole district, monitor implementation and effectiveness, and ensure the provision of ongoing professional development. Chapter 3 will explain more about the role of District Data Teams (DDTs).

Data Teams at the Building Level

The purpose of the Building Data Teams (BDTs) is the same as for the other Data Teams: to improve instructional practice and student learning. The team consists of the principal, representation from each department or grade level, teacher leaders, teacher union representatives, and any other opinion leaders. This team models inquiry by engaging in data-driven decision making that focuses on the implementation of shared instructional practices and the teacher-based Instructional Data Teams (IDTs). The Building Data Teams (BDTs) examine the formative, summative, and monitoring data collected at the school level. They also ensure the alignment of district and building goals, curriculum, and resources in the school improvement planning process. The Building Data Team (BDT) is constructed and led by the principal, and together the team members plan, implement, and monitor the improvement efforts of the school.

Data Teams at the Teacher (Instructional) Level

Instructional Data Teams (IDTs) are small grade-level, department, course, or like-content teams that examine work generated from a common formative assessment. Instructional Data Teams generally use academic Priority Standards (Power Standards) (Ainsworth, 2003a) as a leverage point. The Instructional Data Teams (IDTs) meet a minimum of every two to three weeks and use an explicit data-driven structure for every meeting. In this meeting teachers disaggregate data, analyze student performance, set incremental goals, engage in dialogue around explicit and deliberate instruction, and create a plan to monitor student learning and teacher instruction. Instructional Data Teams (IDTs) are usually facilitated by a teacher-leader, and the effectiveness of the collaboration and the results are monitored by the team, the leader, and the school principal(s).

In Chapter 5 you'll learn more about the foundational components of an Instructional Data Team (IDT).

When Michael Fullan (2008b) talks about school principals leaving legacies, he reminds us that "effective principals spend their time creating the conditions for teachers and teacher leaders to zero-in on effective instructional practices, and to use data on student learning both as a lever for improvement and as a source for external accountability." Data Teams provide the environment for teachers to have rich dialogue around teaching and learning.

DATA AND COLLABORATION: A MARRIAGE OF EFFECTIVE PRACTICES

Many of our colleagues use the phrase, "We are a PLC; we do Data Teams." Professional Learning Communities and Data Teams are not competitive

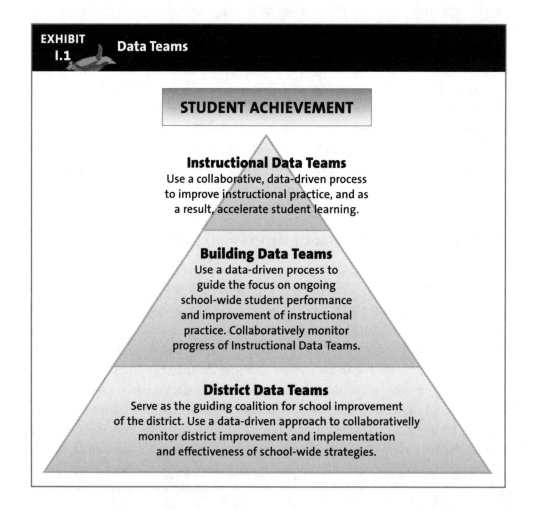

EXHIBIT 1.1   Data Teams

STUDENT ACHIEVEMENT

Instructional Data Teams
Use a collaborative, data-driven process to improve instructional practice, and as a result, accelerate student learning.

Building Data Teams
Use a data-driven process to guide the focus on ongoing school-wide student performance and improvement of instructional practice. Collaboratively monitor progress of Instructional Data Teams.

District Data Teams
Serve as the guiding coalition for school improvement of the district. Use a data-driven approach to collaborativelly monitor district improvement and implementation and effectiveness of school-wide strategies.

practices; they are interdependent practices. The PLC grounds teams in the process of collaboration and inquiry, and the Data Teams process enhances PLCs by providing an explicit, data-driven structure that leads to results.

Stephen White (2005) describes the essential principles of a systematic data-driven process: antecedents, accountability, and collaboration. These principles are embedded in the Data Teams process at every level and are described in the next three sections.

Antecedents

"Antecedents of excellence are measurable indicators of leadership, teaching practices, curriculum, parental involvement, and other factors that influence results" (Reeves, 2006). "Antecedents" are strategies that precede student achievement outcomes. Educators measure the effectiveness and impact of their strategies; they collect cause data. Data Teams have deliberate, explicit conversations around antecedents—or practices—because it is a formal part of the Data Teams process. Data Teams also measure the results, or impact, of their work through the use of assessment results, surveys, observations, and inventories. In this sense Data Teams receive formative feedback as a result of their implementation of strategies to impact learning; they collect cause data. And because of this, Data Teams can easily identify which antecedents, or practices, are effective and allow for replication, celebration, and encouragement for educators to stay the course. By collecting data on their strategies formatively, Data Teams are also able to make midcourse corrections if the data show that a practice is not having the desired impact on teaching and learning. Effective Data Teams, at all three levels, measure and monitor the impact of their strategies.

According to Reeves (2006), "Only by evaluating both causes and effects in a comprehensive accountability system can leaders, teachers, and policymakers understand the complexities of student achievement and the efficacy of teaching and leadership." Exhibit I.2, The Leadership and Learning Matrix, is a visual representation of both results and actions. The vertical axis represents results, most often measured from student assessments. The horizontal axis of the matrix reflects research-based strategies in teaching and leadership. This tool allows us to see a correlation with our actions and their impact on student learning. In Reeves's initial work (2002), he refers to the lack of collecting student achievement data as "malpractice" and challenges us to think of this when we fail to measure leadership actions.

**EXHIBIT
1.2**　　**The Leadership and Learning Matrix**

Effects/Results	**Lucky** High results, low understanding of antecedents Replication of success unlikely	**Leading** High results, high understanding of antecedents Replication of success likely
	Losing Ground Low results, low understanding of antecedents Replication of failure likely	**Learning** Low results, high understanding of antecedents Replication of mistakes unlikely

Antecedents/Cause (Adult Actions)

Accountability

Professional collaboration requires time, practice, and accountability (Reeves, 2009). Educators embrace accountability by embracing Data Teams. Accountability is teacher driven and student centered (Reeves, 2004). "Accountability is the authority to act, permission to subtract, and the responsibility for results" (White, 2005). Educators often associate the term "accountability" with state test scores. However, Data Teams are teacher driven and student centered. Teams use the Data Teams structure to create a plan of action focused on the improvement of instruction, leadership, and student learning, all driven by formative data around student learning and instructional practices.

Earl and Katz (2006) encourage us to think differently about data and accountability. They recommend that instead of housing data within an accountability system, data should be seen as the accountability system itself. In traditional school systems, accountability is seen as a top–down approach in which teachers are the recipients of accountability. Data Teams embrace a bottom–up approach in which the accountability process is embedded in collaborative conversations and shared accountability. In fact, Earl and Katz (2006) say that accountability is more than the use of assessment information; professional accountability is also about making informed decisions using data regarding adult actions.

Collaboration

From White (2005) we have learned that collaboration is necessary to ensure that all viewpoints and voices are heard. White also explains that, through collaboration, we get "beyond the numbers." When we collaboratively analyze data, it becomes meaningful, helps us make better decisions, and helps us make a direct connection between the strategies we are using and the outcomes we are getting. Structured collaboration breaks down the barriers of isolation by creating conditions for open dialogue, honest discussion, and even a dose of healthy debate.

Collaboration should be built into every data-driven decision that we make; in fact, it is the thread of decision-making processes. Schmoker (1999) says, "We must take advantage of data's capacity to prompt collaborative dialogue." The beauty of Data Teams is just that—data provide for a focused, collaborative dialogue. Conversations are not driven by excuses and complaints. Teams collaboratively and enthusiastically work toward a common goal, select common strategies, and celebrate results—together.

Schmoker (1999) also says that the combination of meaningful, informed teamwork; clear, measurable goals; and regular collection and analysis of performance data provide the foundation for results.

PROFESSIONAL LEARNING COMMUNITIES AND DATA TEAMS—WHAT'S THE DIFFERENCE?

Everyone's "doing" PLCs—elementary schools, middle schools, high schools, the central office staff, and even board members. We're all meeting and we're all talking. But what exactly are educators talking about? In fact, Fullan (2008b) claims that the term "PLC" "travels faster than the concept." In other words, PLCs tend to become an initiative, not a process that is intended to change the culture of a school by transforming teaching and leadership.

"The most promising strategy for sustained, substantive school improvement is developing the ability of the school to function as professional learning communities" (DuFour, et al., 1998). The PLC movement has made a tremendous impact on educators, because it was the first major reform effort that caused a shift from professional isolation (also known as "private practice") to professional collaboration (or shared practice). In *Professional Learning Communities at Work* (1998), DuFour, DuFour, and Eaker identified the six characteristics of a PLC:

1. Shared mission, vision, and values

2. Collective inquiry

3. Collaborative teams

4. Action orientated and experimentation

5. Continuous improvement

6. Results orientation

The authors revised the list in 2008 (*Revisiting Professional Learning Communities*) to include the criteria of a focus on goals and learning, and a focus on best instructional practices. They also noted a greater emphasis on "learning by doing" and "commitments" to continuous improvement. Therefore, PLCs are meant to be action oriented.

The PLC structure asks educators to respond to the following questions: What is it we want all students to learn? How will we know when each student has mastered the essential learning? How will we respond when a student experiences initial difficulty in learning? How will we deepen the learning for students who have already mastered essential knowledge and skills (Dufour, et al., 1998)? These questions allow teams to have structured dialogue around curriculum, standards, assessment, and instruction.

Educators have embraced the concept of PLCs as a powerful effort to reform education. PLCs are structured to ensure that all kids are learning.

In education, collaboration often begins with the birth of a PLC. Many leaders have embraced PLCs and have seen the benefits. Teachers began talking to one another and held conversations about student learning. Conversations were often driven by inquiry, and teachers took the opportunity to share instructional strategies. Teachers walked away from the meetings and returned in a few weeks to continue with the same type of dialogue. Good things happened within their PLCs, but their effectiveness moved to the next level when they started "doing Data Teams."

While there are many benefits in having PLCs, the gains in terms of outcomes dramatically increase when these teams infuse the Data Teams process. In the following chapters you will learn more about the Data Teams process at the district, building, and instructional levels. These Data Teams are rich in research and have the results to prove their effectiveness.

Data Teams help schools and districts become results driven. Schools, grade levels, departments, and districts use Data Teams as a vehicle to improve teaching, learning, leadership, and, most of all, student performance. Schmoker (2006) talks about the dividends of the "right kind of teacher collaboration"—its simple, immediate gains in teaching, learning, leadership, and student outcomes. Data Teams are the "right kind" of continuous collaboration.

CHAPTER 1

The Importance of Data for Leadership and Learning

This text is about developing broad and sustained leadership throughout schools and districts by providing focused learning opportunities and shared accountability. The improvement framework is outlined in Chapter 2; however, it is important here to understand that the desired outcome of the improvement framework is a process of continuous improvement for teachers, support staff, and administrators at all levels of the system. This is achieved by creating an improvement focus, learning opportunities and expectations, and specific structures and processes to monitor, assess, and support ongoing progress.

Because this text is about learning systems and data, we thought we would begin with a short personal assessment of your own leadership effectiveness. Specifically, we want to explore how confident you are in your ability to lead your organization (or school or district) to better outcomes.

Let's start with two simple questions:

1. Are you making measurable progress as a building or district? How do you know this? What evidence do you have? Do you know why you are making progress?

2. If you are not making measurable progress, do you know why? What is it that is not working? Which specific actions, strategies, or programs are not working? Do you know why? Do you know what to do to change this?

Take a minute and see if you can answer the first question. List any data or evidence that you have. Can you clearly articulate why you are making progress? This should not be a list of initiatives, unless you know which ones are working and why. Your answer should identify what the adults have done differently—which specific teaching and leadership actions have been taken to "cause" these gains. If you know which adult actions were taken, do you know how to replicate them? Have you been able to replicate this success?

When you're finished, review your list. If you were able to identify the specific adult actions that resulted in success, then you have a significantly higher likelihood of being able to replicate that success. If you cannot identify the adult actions that resulted in the gains, then you're not clear why you made progress.

In answering the second question, do you know what is not working and why? Again, if you cannot articulate what is not working, you don't know what to *stop* doing. If you don't know *why* it is not working, then you do not know how to fix it.

Many districts and buildings can identify some actions that they "think" or "believe" are working, but usually they cannot answer the question regarding "why" they are working. People usually respond with broad generalities like, "that team works well together" or, "I think it is due to the new math program," but most educators struggle to identify a causal relationship between changes in their own actions and the outcomes for the school or district. Without this level of understanding, it is extremely difficult to attribute success or to repeat it. The same holds true for our lack of progress. If we cannot link the actions and the outcomes, we are guessing at best.

Perhaps we believe that if we just keep trying every new initiative or strategy, something will "stick." Sometimes you might be lucky enough that something positive actually does happen, but if you can't accurately connect what it is that you did, or why it happened, you have no hope of repeating this success. In the Leadership and Learning Matrix (Exhibit I.2), Reeves (2006) identifies this phenomenon as being in the "lucky" quadrant (you are making progress but you don't know why), or worse, you are in the "losing" quadrant (you are not making progress and you don't know why).

In addition to understanding more clearly what is working or not, it is also important that everyone understand the connection between their own actions and the outcomes that you are getting. When we don't think that our actions matter, we tend to blame the results on external factors like the students, families, community, district, or even other staff members. One of the reasons why this book focuses on data is because data can help us see the direct relationship between our own actions and the outcomes we're getting. This book is focused on identifying and learning about which actions make a measurable difference in the performance of our schools and districts. There are a number of overarching ideas associated with this work.

BIG IDEAS

The following Big Ideas will help you understand and be able to implement specific actions that will help you in the data-driven inquiry and improvement process.

1. Teachers and leaders matter in terms of the outcomes that students are getting.

2. It is what teachers and leaders *do* that matters the most.

3. Schools and districts get better outcomes when they focus and learn from that focus.

4. The primary focus should be on instruction.

5. Implementation, monitoring, feedback, and support all matter.

6. Data should provide a starting point and focus for your actions, help assess your progress, and identify where you are being successful and where there is a need for more support.

7. Schools and districts, acting in alignment as a system, make improvements through data-driven inquiry and continuous learning.

8. Teams help us inquire, learn more deeply, provide more effective guidance in terms of support, and provide opportunities for developing leadership, ownership, and accountability across the district.

You will see these Big Ideas reflected throughout this text. The data-driven inquiry and improvement procedure should also result in greater leadership and learning opportunities across the school system.

THE USE OF TEAMS

Making systemic improvement requires instructional leadership across the entire district. We recommend doing this through the use of teams at each level of the system, a District Data Team (DDT), a Building Data Team (BDT), and an Instructional Data Team (IDT). While the formation and use of these teams is important, it is what the teams do that matters the most. Without a team at each level, we do not have the opportunity to collectively learn at each level and provide appropriate feedback and support across the system. Of all three levels of teams (district, building, and instructional), the most powerful teams are the teacher-based Instructional Data Teams (IDTs), which examine and act on student and teacher learning in an ongoing way. Without a Building Data Team

(BDT), however, it is difficult to develop or sustain effective teams across the whole school. The same holds true at the school district level. Without a District Data Team (DDT), it is difficult to evaluate progress, to identify and replicate successful practices, or to generate and provide the necessary supports that are needed to sustain effective schools across the entire district.

We have struggled for years with fits and starts, looking for the "one program" or strategy (or silver bullet) that will make "the difference," only to be disappointed again and again. It is no wonder that teachers and administrators are skeptical about the next new thing. This continues to happen because we have not been engaged in a systemic or systematic way to make improvements across the entire school system. To make system-wide progress, we need to engage in a process that shares responsibility and accountability widely across each school and the entire district. To address this, we recommend the development of Data Teams at the three different levels discussed in the preceding paragraph:

1. District-level Data Team

2. Building-level Data Team

3. Instructional (teacher-based) Data Team

Each of these teams has a specific purpose and function of its own; however, the teams also have a "reciprocal" relationship with one another, such that their success is tied to one another (Elmore, 2004). The teams operate in a way where "we are not successful if you are not successful." We will describe in greater detail the specific roles and responsibilities of each of these teams in Section Two.

IMPROVEMENT FRAMEWORK

While the improvement framework will be addressed in greater detail in Chapter 2, the framework is based on the core concept that if districts and buildings are truly going to make continuous progress, they will need to focus their improvement efforts and learn from them. The framework includes six components:

1. Use data in an ongoing way.

2. Limit the number of goals and strategies, then focus on them.

3. Develop shared instructional practices.

4. Implement deeply.

5. Monitor, provide feedback, and render support.

6. Learn through inquiry.

What may not be immediately evident from reading the components of the framework is that *instructional improvement is at the core of all of this work.*

Focus on Instruction

The following quote by Richard Elmore (2004, p. 66) should act as the cornerstone for all of the improvement work in the schools and the district: "The purpose of leadership is the improvement of instructional practice and performance, regardless of role." If the work that we do does not result in improving instruction in the classroom, it may be interesting, and even important, but it is not critical to improvement. Providing instructional leadership should be everyone's responsibility, "regardless of role." While most building and district administrators give lip service to this concept, what we know is that "direct involvement in instruction is among the least frequent activities performed by administrators of any kind at any level" (Elmore, 2004, p. 48). Elmore goes on to say that "instructional improvement requires continuous learning" (p. 67). The district-wide work to improve outcomes for every student in every subgroup is never complete; it requires ongoing, continuous improvement at every level of the system. It also requires that we have a procedure that allows us to learn from our successes and a way of assessing and providing supports when individuals and teams are not making progress.

EDUCATIONAL LEADERSHIP
AND IMPROVEMENT

Most leaders at the building and district levels would identify themselves as "change agents." They perceive themselves to be open to and embracing of ongoing change. The reality, however, is that when most people talk about being change leaders or change agents, they are really talking about other people changing, not themselves. There is little personal risk associated with asking other people to change when we do not change ourselves. The maxim that leaders must personally embrace is, "If you want different outcomes, lead differently!" The most effective way to lead differently is to provide better instructional leadership, from the superintendent on down, by learning more about instruction and improvement and expecting everyone else to do the same.

This book is about leading differently. It is about leading and deeply implementing a focused, instructional improvement agenda while learning individually and collectively. It is also about developing greater instructional leadership capacity across the entire school district through the effective use of data-based teams at every level.

IMPLEMENTATION AND SUPPORT

Before we begin reviewing the framework in Chapter 2, we will discuss three other topics related to successful change:

    1. The implementation gap: Why don't we follow through?

    2. What can we do to deepen our implementation?

       • Focus on the content of improvement.

       • Use a top–down and bottom–up approach for learning.

       • Facilitate the rate of change.

    3. Leadership pressure and support.

The Implementation Gap

We are now a decade into the 21st century. Yet, looking at schools today, many people would say that schools have not changed significantly from a hundred years ago. According to Hayes-Jacobs (2010, pp. 60–61), "The overwhelming majority of our schools run on the same length of the school year and same daily schedule, with the same rigid grouping of students, and the same faculty organizations, and fundamentally the same type of buildings as in the late 1890s." Others say that schools change "promiscuously (but) without producing any improvement" (Elmore, 2004 , p. 104). Schools seem to change direction and programs frequently and randomly but without challenging many of the structures and processes that keep us right where we are. To paraphrase Einstein, it is insane to expect different outcomes from the same practices, no matter how hard we try.

In any case, most people would agree that schools and districts have struggled to implement meaningful, long-term improvements. While there are exceptions, the majority of schools and districts are still struggling to bring up overall improvement or make any significant or sustainable gains for specific subgroups.

While there are multiple reasons for this lack of progress (the wrong strategies, processes, and leadership, to name a few), the single most predictable problem is the lack of follow-through at all levels of the system. In our work with hundreds of districts and buildings across the country, we have consistently identified the lack of follow-through as the single biggest factor associated with the lack of progress for districts and buildings. We've come to call this the "implementation gap." Interestingly, this lack of follow-through is not usually related to a lack of knowledge (people know what to do), but rather a lack of execution. For example, we have known for some time that most educators (teachers and administrators) know more about effective practice than they regularly use in their work (Sparks, 2005). This lack of follow-through is not limited to teachers but is endemic to the entire system. We all know more about effective practices than we regularly use.

Teacher Follow-Through

To highlight this problem, let's begin with teacher follow-through. Wiliam (2007), like many other researchers, found that the difference between the most effective classrooms and least effective classrooms was attributable to the teacher. However, he also found that the difference between the most effective teachers and least effective teachers is not what they *know*, but rather what they *do*. He says that if we are serious about raising achievement, we need to help teachers change what they do in classrooms (i.e., implement more effective teaching practices). This finding is particularly interesting, because the usual fallback position when people aren't implementing is to assume that they need more professional development. In fact, what they really need is more practice and support in implementing (e.g., more practice in applying successful methods in the classroom, more modeling, more coaching, and more observations: see Reeves, 2010). Pfeffer and Sutton (2000) recommend that we focus less on providing more formal training programs and more on actually doing the work (i.e., multiple opportunities for practice). Interestingly, there is a similar finding between teachers and students in that "it is what teachers get students to do in the class that emerges as the strongest component of the accomplished teacher's repertoire (Hattie, 2009, p. 35). This problem cannot be attributed to just teachers, however, as we have found this to be a systems problem. For teachers, follow-through has to do with implementing the focused instructional practices in their classrooms and following through in their Instructional Data Teams (IDTs).

Administrator Follow-Through

When it comes to most administrators, it is difficult to even say that we have a focus or priority on instruction because so little of our time is spent in this area. Elmore (2004) found that "direct involvement in instruction is among the least frequent activities performed by administrators of any kind at any level, and those who do engage in instructional leadership activities on a consistent basis are a relatively small proportion of the total administrative force" (p. 48). So if instructional improvement is important, then it must have a higher priority, and administrators at every level must act more on this priority.

The first major hurdle, then, is to establish instruction as the highest priority for everyone. In our work with districts and buildings, the first way that we usually assess this priority is to ask administrators to conduct a simple time audit and to determine how much time they spend in classrooms every day or are directly involved in other instructional issues. When administrators collect data on the actual amount of time they spend in these activities over one week, they typically find that the time is significantly less than the estimated amount.

Most administrators agree that if instruction is to have the priority, they should commit to a minimum of at least one hour per day. While part of this time should be dedicated to the Building Data Teams (BDTs) and Instructional Data Teams (IDTs), the other time should be spent in classrooms conducting observations and walk-throughs and providing feedback. Many superintendents who have realigned their priorities toward instruction have found it more realistic to schedule one day per week to focus on instruction. This may seem like a high standard to set for superintendents, but districts that have made significant progress found that their participation on the District Data Team (DDT) and time spent in schools and classrooms resulted in higher performance across the schools in the district. Some districts have completely realigned their central offices in such a way that all of the central office staff members are focused on supporting instruction in the buildings (Honig, et al., 2010).

For administrators, therefore, the follow-through has more to do with monitoring the instructional practices and providing feedback and support.

In looking at principals, Duke (2007) found that the difference between more effective and less effective principals was not their commitment to specific reform initiatives but rather their level of follow-through and monitoring. Unlike teachers, we don't expect principals to implement the instructional practices themselves but to ensure that staff members are effectively implementing the practices. Therefore, the principal's implementation responsibilities are more related to monitoring teacher follow-through and providing feedback, guidance, and supports like mentoring, coaching, and opportunities for observation.

Murphy and Hallinger (1988) and Marzano and Waters (2009) made similar findings for the superintendent and central office staff. They found that more successful districts had superintendents and central office staff that actively monitored, evaluated, and provided feedback on the implementation of their curricular and instructional initiatives, including the quality of research-based instructional practices. These districts also used ongoing *formative* indicators to measure both their level of implementation and the impact of their efforts on student achievement.

When districts begin their efforts to monitor the levels of implementation and the impact of their strategies on student learning, they are often initially dismayed at the lack of implementation at the classroom level. Changing classroom practices takes more than just monitoring the level of implementation; it also takes feedback and differentiated levels of support. As Bossidy and Charan (2002) caution, "Leadership without the discipline of execution is incomplete and ineffective" (p. 34).

If you walk away with only one lesson from this text, it should be this:

We close the achievement gap
by
closing the implementation gap.

Why Don't We Implement Well?

While there is no shortage of reasons as to why we don't implement well, we want to explore a few of the more important ones here. First of all, there are simply too many priorities to address them all successfully. When faced with a multitude of priorities, people become overwhelmed and tend to focus on what they think they can accomplish and be successful at. Later in this book we will talk about the importance of limiting the number of goals and strategies and focusing on those strategies as a critical first step in helping people follow through. However, even when school and district leaders do limit and focus their goals and strategies, they still find it extremely difficult to achieve deep implementation in every school and classroom. One reason is because district and school leaders uniformly overestimate the effectiveness of their traditional professional development efforts.

Even when leaders understand that there is a need to provide more follow-up learning and support, they often aren't quite sure what to provide or how to provide it. District and school staff members often seem perplexed when we ask them to learn from their experiences and take the work deeper. People often take the position that "We've done what we were supposed to do, but other people haven't done what they were supposed to do." The idea of using the chain of command to hold someone else responsible may be the norm, but it only contributes to the problem.

Instead, we need to link everyone's responsibilities and success to everyone else's responsibilities and success. We need tighter accountability between each level of the system, where we hold each other responsible for either effective follow-through or requests for more support. The idea of "reciprocal accountability" (Elmore, 2004) is that the system should be designed in such a way that all of the adults are responsible for developing the capacity and performance of each other.

If specific schools are not making progress, it is the District Data Team's responsibility to work with the Building Data Team (BDT) to strengthen the success of individual staff members or the teams, not just "kick the dog" or "fire the principal," which seems to be the current federal solution. The same holds true at the building level. If the building is not making progress at every grade level, or in every department or course, it is the responsibility of the principal to work with the Building Data Team (BDT) to generate alternative strategies or supports and to work with staff to implement the strategies or supports. It is also the Building Data Team's responsibility to work with the District Data Team (DDT) to develop the strategies and then garner the necessary resources and supports to implement and evaluate the strategies. Everyone must share responsibility and accountability to develop the system-wide capacity to be more effective.

If you are not making progress, it is your job to get support. It is the responsibility of the District Data Team (DDT) or the Building Data Team (BDT) to make sure that you get that support. The message from everyone must be, "It is my job to make sure that you and your team are successful."

This approach runs counter to the prevailing practice, where we expect (or rather pretend) that everyone should have all of the knowledge and skills that they need. Consequently, everyone puts forth a false bravado. In our approach, it is expected that individuals and teams will actively seek help and support when they are struggling to make progress. Consequently, no one is in this alone unless you don't follow through or request support.

The framework is designed to help people focus and learn from their work. The idea of holding everyone responsible for learning creates a different form of accountability, one in which we are mutually responsible for each other's success. This concept of "reciprocal accountability" also involves monitoring the levels of implementation and then providing feedback and support to staff in a timely fashion. The most important part for each team, however, is learning which strategies and supports are the most effective, with which staff, in which contexts. Systems that are successful systematically involve everyone in learning how to successfully implement new and more powerful teaching and leadership practices.

What Can We Do to Deepen Our Learning and Implementation?

Deepening our learning and implementation across the whole organization (school or district) poses a great challenge to most school systems. To be effective, we need to lead the learning and implementation differently. The following information discusses specific ways to think about implementing more deeply.

In terms of schools and districts, there are only three primary levels of change: curriculum, instruction, and assessment.

Curriculum

Curriculum updating is often a constant process in districts. While we will not go into great detail here, it is appropriate for districts to examine their curriculum in relation to state and national standards. However, as a result, most districts have ended up with a curriculum that is too broad, with too many topics and not enough guidance in terms of focus. Darling-Hammond (2010) states that our "*transmission-oriented curriculum* was designed to be delivered in the large impersonal factory-model schools" (p. 5; emphasis added). She says that "creating thoughtful standards, useful curriculum guidance, and generative assessments will require a number of changes from current practice in the United States" (p. 293).

Countries that have significantly improved across all of their subgroups have gone in a different direction than we have in the United States. "Teachers in high-achieving nations take several months to ensure that students learn a given topic deeply and from many different angles ... by contrast, the U.S. custom of rushing through dozens of textbook topics each year—made worse by the demands of current tests in many states—means that students 'cover' topics (but are) unable to apply these topics easily to real problems" (Darling-Hammond, 2010, p. 298). She concludes by saying, "Higher achieving countries have much leaner standards; teach fewer topics more deeply each year; focus more on inquiry, reasoning skills, and application of knowledge, rather than mere coverage; and have a more thoughtful sequence of expectations based on developmental learning progressions within and across domains" (p. 285). We still have a long way to go and much to learn in the area of curriculum development from other countries that have been more successful at raising performance for all of their students.

While many districts have gone through the hard work of "unwrapping" standards to identify the Big Ideas and Essential Questions, and aligning their curriculum behind these Power Standards, many have not. This work of "unwrapping" and identifying Power Standards, also referred to as Priority Standards, is important work at the district level, and, once this hard work has been done, the district curriculum needs to be the "taught curriculum." This is part of what Marzano (2003) refers to as a "guaranteed and viable" curriculum.

It is not our intent here to outline a process for curriculum development or reform except to say that there is still important work to be done by most districts. Most districts still need to develop and implement a more focused, sequenced, and integrated curriculum that involves fewer topics, more inquiry, and more real-world applications.

Instruction and Assessment

From what we have discussed, it is obvious that what matters the most is the teacher, and what the teacher actually does. Simply put, more effective teachers regularly use more effective teaching practices. So if you want better outcomes, you need to strengthen the quality of instruction.

Strengthening Teacher Practice

While many district and building leaders intuitively understand the importance of strengthening teacher practice—and may have even focused on trying to change what teachers do in classrooms—most leaders have found this to be extremely complex and challenging work. Part of this challenge is due to the fact that teachers naturally gravitate toward approaches that are similar to their current practices (Stein and Coburn, 2008). Because change is difficult, we all tend to favor changes that are closer to what we already know or do now, or to adopt incremental changes that don't require too much new learning.

Acquiring and implementing new practices that are difficult or complex require new major learning or making changes that appear antithetical to current practices. New learning often requires "unlearning" what you already know or believe, and according to Richard Elmore, this can "work against the development of new more effective practices" (Fullan, 2008a). This is sometimes referred to as "second-order change" (Marzano, Waters, and McNulty, 2005) because it requires us to examine our current beliefs and unlearn what we already do.

One of the most important ways to address the challenges associated with second-order change is to create a direct connection for teachers between their implementation of the new practices and the impact that the practices have on student learning. While no one would argue that student background makes a difference in student performance, what matters more is what the teacher does in the classroom. Leaders at all levels need to help make the explicit connection between specific teaching practices and the outcomes for students. We will discuss this topic again later when we talk about Data Teams, but it is important to understand that leaders need to effectively use data to help make the connection between the teacher's actions and the students' outcomes.

In addition to using data, what else can leaders do to positively affect the use of new and more powerful teaching practices? Certainly they can use their positional authority and exert some pressure to use the new practices, but usually external pressure, by itself, is insufficient to motivate teachers to change their current practices. For example, in a survey of more than 320 teachers, Salmonowicz (2009) found that even in the face of losing their current positions, teachers didn't see the need to change the way that they were teaching.

What does help then? Weinbaum and Supovitz (2010) found that teachers were more likely to change their practices when they felt that there was a compelling reason to change. The specific reasons they identified were:

1. Staff felt that the changes were central to their own work and the work of the rest of the staff.

2. The changes identified would address an issue that school staff perceived to be a real issue or problem.

3. Staff could see or be provided with early evidence of effectiveness of the practices being proposed.

Given these findings, leaders should consider what they can do to create a compelling case to address all three of these issues. To do this, we recommend that you implement the improvement framework outlined in Chapter 2. As you will see, the focus of the framework is on instructional improvement that includes an approach to learning about instruction and implementing more powerful instructional practices. The District Data Team (DDT), the Building Data Team (BDT), and the Instructional Data Team (IDT) are all focused on learning and implementing more powerful instructional practices that address the unique learning needs of students and that demonstrate gains in success for all students.

LEARNING AND IMPROVING INSTRUCTION

Top–Down and Bottom–Up Learning

Recently we have learned quite a bit about the improvement process as it relates to school systems. While there are many approaches to improving schools and districts, some approaches have proved to be more effective than others. At its core, the improvement process must focus on instruction and create opportunities for focused, ongoing learning at every level. What we (and others; see Chrispeels, et al., 2008) have found to be most effective involves both top–down and bottom–up strategies. Collectively, learning to use more effective research-based practices and simultaneously learning as a part of data-based teams, we work together to strengthen the connection between teacher actions and student performance. One without the other is insufficient. Jacobson (2010) recently raised the question of whether it was possible to work on both coherent instructional improvements and PLCs simultaneously. If not, he argues that neither is strong enough alone to result in continuous improvement.

We believe that it is not only possible but preferable to work on both. We accomplish this through two primary strategies:

1. Learning to appropriately and effectively use specific research-based teaching practices.

2. Using data-based teams for continuous learning.

These two strategies are explained in greater detail in subsequent chapters; however, an overview is provided here.

Top–Down: Creating a Focus on Learning Specific Teaching Practices

At the district level, there will always be some continuing need for learning specific practices on a district-wide basis. Whether this includes strategies from the district literacy plan, specific strategies associated with the new math curriculum, or the selection of specific, effective teaching practices (like clear learning outcomes), the point is that there will always be the need to develop some shared practices across the district.

In addition, Jacobson (2010) argues that districts and buildings need more than just PLCs: "DuFour and his collaborators expect that analyzing common assessments leads to collaboration on how to teach differently. Yet in this model instructional innovation comes about *primarily* as teachers *react* to their analysis of assessment results" (p. 40). Jacobson goes on to make the case that these teams tend to rely on practices that they already know and use and that there is a need to infuse new and more powerful practices into the work of these teams.

Our approach addresses both—the power of teams, paired with everyone learning new, powerful instructional strategies. This allows the District Data Team (DDT) and the Building Data Teams (BDTs) to study both individual learning (powerful instructional practices) and collective learning (district, building, and teacher-based teams) and then learn from both efforts.

To achieve more powerful teaching, we need to use more powerful teaching practices. Given this reality, there are three overriding questions that the district needs to answer:

1. What teaching or instructional practices should we all focus on to learn together?

2. How well can we, or do we, implement and learn the practices?

3. Do the instructional practices make a difference in student learning?

No one seems to doubt that if we want to improve student performance, we need teachers to learn and use more powerful teaching practices. In the last few years, strong research has focused on what more effective teaching looks like (see the Chapter 2 discussion on Darling-Hammond, et al., 2008; Wahlstrom and Louis, 2008). In addition, several meta-analytic studies identified specific instructional strategies that can have a profound effect on students and their learning. (Also see Chapter 3, discussion on Marzano, et al., 2001; Hattie, 2009.)

While this research has been extremely valuable in helping to develop consensus on what more powerful instruction looks like, there is still concern regarding how to support teachers to appropriately and effectively use these practices. Levin (2008) says that effective change in schools comes from the "thoughtful application of effective practices in particular contexts" (p. 81). It isn't enough to just learn the practices if we don't know how and when to use them appropriately.

Marzano (2009) recently cautioned, "While beginning with a narrow focus is legitimate, a school or district must expand the breadth of its discussion of effective teaching" (p. 32). He also states that "focusing on any single set of categories exclusively is a serious mistake.... The entire constellation of strategies is necessary for a complete view of effective teaching.... The important message here is that providing feedback to teachers regarding effective instruction necessitates articulating a broad array of strategies organized into a comprehensive framework" (pp. 31–32).

Marzano's caution is important. If districts or schools are seen as randomly picking instructional strategies simply based on the research or effect size (or percent increase in student performance), and then expect to see them all the time in every classroom, it only reinforces teachers' skepticism that has developed from too many ill-thought-out and poorly implemented initiatives. However, it is important for teachers to learn new and more powerful teaching strategies to add to their repertoires. So where does the balance lie here?

A focus on specific teaching practices is appropriate when everyone understands that the strategies are part of the broader instructional framework and that for "learning purposes" we are focusing on only a part of the broader instructional framework. A district or building can "begin developing a language of instruction by focusing on a list of instructional strategies, management strategies, or assessment strategies. But this is just a beginning ... the common language of instruction should become part of discussion and feedback with teachers.... Both discussion and feedback are critical to developing expertise" (Marzano, 2009, p. 35).

It is appropriate, therefore, at the district and/or building level, to develop a focused learning agenda that includes specific teaching and assessment practices that are learned over time as part of a broader instructional framework. This idea of targeting specific practices and then phasing them in over time has growing support in the research literature in education and other fields as well (Leithwood and Jantzi, 2008; Bossidy and Charan, 2002; Patterson, et al., 2008). Knight (2009) found that professional learning is more effective when it is focused on a few critically important practices that are implemented successfully. Senge (1990) states that "small, well-focused actions can sometimes produce significant, enduring improvements if they are in the right place" (p. 64).

The idea of extrapolating small experiences to larger settings is not new. The idea of self-repeating patterns, or microcosms, has been around since the Greeks (e.g., Socrates, Plato, and Pythagoras). This idea can be extended to systems thinking when we ask, "Can the system learn?" By examining the ability of the system to learn small, cumulative learning tasks, we can examine the overall ability of the system to learn or not.

Parsley and Galvin (2008) refer to these as "fractal improvement experiences." They recommend that "the focus of the fractal experience should have broad impact and require wide participation by staff members, yet be narrow enough to implement and see results in a short period of time" (pp. 4–5). They recommend that these small fractal experiences be a part of the larger learning agenda of the school and of the improvement cycle. They elaborate by saying, "Given the prevailing culture of independent practice, it is not uncommon to find school faculties who have *never* experienced measurable success that they attribute to working together as a team. Changing the culture of a school to one of shared responsibility and collective action is foundational to improvement, but is a complex and lengthy process. Engaging in a fractal experience provides a vehicle for a school staff to begin changing the culture of their school while making real, measurable gains for students in a short period of time" (p. 5).

They go on to discuss how such fractal experiences can assist in the development of "collective efficacy" or collective effectiveness across all of the staff. We will talk more about this later, but the goal should be the development of shared effectiveness or "collective efficacy" across the school. What we want to instill is the belief that what we do matters, and that we can be successful in meeting the goals we have set, with the students we have.

We came to the same conclusion—that by focusing on small learning experiences, buildings and districts can learn how to learn. District Data Teams (DDTs) and Building Data Teams (BDTs) that study the implementation of small learning experiences can analyze and identify the reasons for the success of individuals, teams, schools, and the district at large. This focused approach allows districts and buildings to study their implementation and to examine how to implement practices deeply into classrooms. Having this focus also allows the teams to study the impact of these practices on student learning.

By focusing, districts and buildings can more effectively monitor their implementation and then provide feedback and support to staff in a timely way. The teams can learn from successful implementation in classrooms and in schools, teasing out the specific factors that helped support successful implementation. The teams can also examine how to replicate these learnings in other settings, allowing for the opportunity to examine how well we learn as a system.

Bottom–Up: Data-Based Learning Teams

If the approach to improvement included only learning specific instructional practices over time, the outcomes would be limited. Along with teachers individually learning to implement new and more effective strategies, there also needs to be ongoing, powerful collective learning through the use of data-based teams at the classroom, school, and district levels. "Because schools are social settings, change is not just a matter of giving people new ideas but of creating social conditions that foster and support changed practices" (Levin, 2008, p. 83).

Most researchers and practitioners would agree that teams are not always the most efficient way to make decisions; however, when we are talking about "systems learning," teams can be both an efficient and effective methodology for learning. As you will see in subsequent chapters, and as discussed elsewhere in this chapter, the structures that we recommend include the district-level Data Team (DDT), the building-level Data Team (BDT), and the teacher-based, or Instructional, Data Team (IDT).

If we are going to reach broad consensus on the problems, the strategies, and the progress we're making (or not), and examine what we can learn and do to improve implementation, it is essential that we create more broad-based opportunities for input, examination, and learning across the system. No single individual has the intellectual capacity, imaginative power, operational ability, and interpersonal skills to move the work forward by himself (Ancona, et al., 2007). Whether we called this distributed leadership, shared leadership, or collaborative leadership, we know from Leithwood, et al. (2007) that school leadership has a greater influence on staff and students when it is widely distributed. We also know that if we want systems to learn, we need to develop many leaders who work together rather than relying only on key individuals in specific positions (Fullan, 2008a; Kotter, 1996).

In Chapter 3 we outline in some detail what the research tells us about highly effective districts. When you review the characteristics of effective districts, what should become clear is that, to carry out these responsibilities you need to distribute or share leadership. The use of teams at the classroom, school, and district levels provides opportunities to develop leadership capacity and shared ownership and accountability for progress at every level.

Murphy and Meyers (2008) found, "There's an extensive body of research and development work on the elements, importance, and effects of teams in organizations, especially on building highly effective work teams" (p. 238). To make systemic improvement district-wide, they recommended the creation and coordination of effective teams at the central office level and all other levels "deep into the organization" (p. 239). They found that the key to effective reform was to change the culture of the classroom, the school, and the district. They also found that the development of teams at each of these levels was essential to changing those cultures. They concluded that to get the best performance from people in schools and districts, the best teamwork needs to be developed at every level.

There is ample evidence regarding the effectiveness of school- and teacher-based Data Teams (Darling-Hammond, 2010; Supovitz, 2006; Reeves, 2007; Weinbaum and Supovitz, 2010; DuFour, et al., 2008). Darling-Hammond (2010) reported that multiple studies have identified the collaboration associated with professional communities of teachers as a key element of effective schools. She stated, "Successful schools continually work to improve the quality of their instruction by making it the consistent focus of their professional learning time" (p. 261). In an earlier work, Darling-Hammond, et al. (2009) reported that in a comprehensive five-year study of more than 1,500 schools, when teachers formed instructional-level Data Teams, achievement increased in math, reading, science, and history, and absentee and dropout rates decreased.

By creating these Instructional Data Teams (IDTs) "that meet regularly, the school creates structures for examining student progress, as well as for creating a more coherent curriculum and allowing teachers to learn from one another" (Darling-Hammond, 2010, p. 261). We will provide greater detail on the functions, roles, and responsibilities for the district-, building-, and instructional-based teams in subsequent chapters.

FACILITATING THE CHANGE PROCESS

Earlier in this chapter we discussed recent research by Weinbaum and Supovitz (2010) that identified reasons why teachers became more engaged with changing their practice. One reason was that they could see early evidence of the effectiveness of the practices. In other words, teachers could see a positive impact on student learning in a short period of time. To address this issue of timeliness, leaders need to know how to move the work forward at a pace so that people can see the results of their work quickly. Fortunately, there is practical guidance on how leaders can help to move the work forward in a timely way.

First, by focusing on specific teaching practices, the new practices can be learned, practiced, and implemented within a manageable period of time. This allows teachers to observe and collect their own formative assessment data on the impact of the strategies on student learning quickly. This also allows the Building Data Team (BDT) to collect data on the implementation of the practices and to examine ongoing student work. The Building Data Team (BDT) should be able to demonstrate the connection between the use of strategies and the quality of student work and then report this back to the rest of the staff.

There is also a robust literature on what helps to support the successful adoption of new practices. Certainly, the seminal text on this work is the *Diffusion of Innovations* by Everett Rogers (1962, 2003). Rogers's work provides a comprehensive theory of how new practices spread across social systems or organizations. Overall, the typical cycle of adoption of new practices looks much like the normal bell curve, where 2.5 percent of the population are classified as innovators, 13.5 percent are early adopters, 34 percent are in both the early majority and late majority categories, and 16 percent are included in what he referred to as the "laggards" category. Rogers also identified five stages that people go through in the adoption process: knowledge, persuasion, decision, implementation, and confirmation.

Rogers also talks about specific characteristics of an innovation and whether or not people perceive that there is more of a personal advantage to using the proposed practice over their current practice. Individuals personally review this "relative advantage" along with other characteristics, including "compatibility," "complexity," "trialability," and "observability," in evaluating whether or not they should adopt the new practice.

While we recommend that you familiarize yourself more deeply with his work, the specific area that we want to focus on here is how to decrease the amount of time it takes to successfully adopt new practices. In Chapter 2 we will discuss the need to focus our improvement efforts by using a limited number of goals and strategies. We will also discuss focusing on specific effective instructional practices that are a part of a broader instructional improvement framework. Each of these is important in itself to help gain a focus, but there are several other strategies that help people see the benefit and effectiveness of using the practices early on. It is important for leaders to understand how to help staff be successful in using the practices to more quickly reach a "critical mass" so that the practices become self-sustaining.

The three most effective strategies to increase the speed of staff using and being successful with the practices are:

1. Providing opportunities for practice and mastery experiences.

2. Using social persuasion or peer pressure through opinion leaders.

3. Reducing people's learning anxieties or psychological fears.

Each of these strategies relates to enhancing the individual's personal belief in his own ability to be successful with the practice, or with his own "self-efficacy" (Bandura, 1997). The bottom line in any change initiative is, "Do I think I can be successful in this task?" Ultimately, our own belief or "self-efficacy" becomes a self-fulfilling prophecy; that is, if we believe we can be successful, we usually are. Unfortunately, the reverse is also true—if we do not believe we will be successful, we usually are not. If we want to have individuals and groups be successful, we need to build both individual and collective effectiveness or efficacy. The following are the most powerful strategies for building individual and collective efficacy and for accelerating the adoption of effective practices.

Opportunities for Practice and Mastery Experiences, and Modeling or "Vicarious Experiences"

Ultimately, the most successful way to help move people forward is to have them experience success in using the practice. Usually, we achieve this by giving them the opportunity to practice the skill over and over again until they reach a level of "mastery." This is why, if we want people to be successful, we often break more complex learning tasks down into more manageable-sized pieces and then provide the opportunity for individuals to practice each of the pieces until they have successfully mastered them. No doubt you've heard the saying "success breeds success." It is true that having successful experiences increases our belief in our own ability, or self-efficacy. According to Patterson, et al. (2008), successful personal experiences are the "gold standard of change" (p. 57). Being successful at a task, however, is directly related to having multiple opportunities to practice the task. Reeves (2010) concluded that effective teaching has everything to do with "deliberate practice." He quotes Willingham (2009), saying that teaching, like any other complex cognitive skills, requires practice to be improved. Reeves identifies the components of deliberate practice as:

1. A focused task,

2. That is practiced over time, and

3. Receives immediate feedback through accurate self-assessment, coaching, or modeling.

Educators often underestimate the amount of time, or number of trials that it takes to effectively learn a new skill. According to different studies, it takes somewhere between 20 to 50 trials (depending on the complexity of the skill) before learners feel relatively confident in using a new practice. This means that we have to provide extended opportunities for practice, paired with feedback, if we really expect people to use new practices effectively.

When individual staff members struggle with the implementation of new practices, they need to receive more support so that they can experience success (e.g., coaching and feedback on how to use the practices more effectively, having the practice modeled by someone else). Observing someone else successfully model the practices provides the opportunity for powerful learning, particularly if the observer identifies with the person whom he is observing. This type of "modeling" is referred to as "vicarious experience" and can be a powerful motivator in helping people persevere in their efforts. With current technologies, it is relatively easy and inexpensive to capture examples of more successful peers on digital videotape or DVD and provide multiple opportunities for observations.

What is important for leaders to understand here is that it is essential for people to have multiple, ongoing opportunities to try implementing specific practices and to experience success from using the practices. If staff members are being successful and seeing results, this is optimal. If staff members are not being successful, however, it is important to intervene and provide them with differential levels of support. Coaching, feedback, classroom observations, or video examples posted on the intranet are all ways to demonstrate the effectiveness of the practices to staff members who need to experience success.

Utilizing Opinion Leaders

Another way we can speed up the adoption process is to involve opinion leaders early in the process and, if possible, have them communicate the benefits of the practices to their peers. Reeves (2008) found that "behavioral change does not follow the creation of a belief system; it precedes it. Behavior stems from an emotional attachment to a trusted colleague. The Gallup organization found that most employees in most organizations take their cues from a trusted colleague, not the boss or the trainer" (p. 62).

Patterson and his colleagues (2008) tell us that "opinion leaders are socially connected and respected. The rest of the population (over 85 percent) will not adopt new practice until opinion leaders do" (p. 148). They go on to say that opinion leaders are both "*respected* and *connected*" and that people pay attention to them because they possess two important qualities:

1. Opinion leaders are seen as knowledgeable about the issue, practice, or content that is being proposed. They are seen as competent professionals.

2. They are *seen as trustworthy* and keep other people's best interest in mind (p. 153).

Patterson, et al. (2008) state that "no resource is more powerful and accessible than the persuasion of the people who make up the social network" (p. 138). Furthermore, when an opinion leader attempts to implement a new practice "and succeeds, this one act alone can go further in motivating others to change than almost any other source of influence" (p. 144).

Opinion leaders have their greatest impact on their coworkers when their peers are going through the process of evaluating the practice themselves, and when they work with people who are the most reluctant to change their practices (the "late adopters"). During both of these times, opinion leaders play a critical role in moving the work forward more expeditiously.

Everyone does not exert an equal amount of influence over the adoption process. Opinion leaders are more influential with their peers both positively and negatively in terms of the advice that they give. Patterson and his colleagues (2008) say that you should "find the opinion leaders, spend a disproportionate amount of time with them, listen to their concerns, build trust with them, be open to their ideas, and rely on them to share your ideas" (p. 151).

The biggest challenge for most leaders is that they do not know who their opinion leaders are. Please be aware that they are not necessarily the most outspoken individuals, nor do they often hold any positional authority. Instead, they are people who are seen as competent and trustworthy. It is well worth the time for leaders to identify these opinion leaders using the dual criteria of technical knowledge and trustworthiness. Once leaders have identified the opinion leaders, they need to systematically involve them in the change initiatives. It is particularly important to get as many opinion leaders as possible on the District Data Team (DDT) and the Building Data Team (BDT) and then to pay attention to their advice.

Reducing Learning Anxieties or Psychological Fears

Teaching is a highly personal activity. When we as leaders ask teachers to make their teaching more public and more accountable, this feels highly personal and potentially very threatening. While the idea of shared practices and shared learning sound good in practice, this induces a high degree of anxiety for many people. Putting our professional competencies on public display in front of our peers is probably the most threatening activity imaginable.

To address this issue, leaders need to lead differently by helping to reduce the learning anxieties that people are experiencing. This is done by providing better structures and processes to carry out the new work (Patterson, et al., 2008). When new learning or changes are being introduced, remember that "structures are your friends." Structures help create a new and different set of interactions and experiences that help people to learn. Using protocols, norms, and processes all help to support different conversations about teaching and learning at a deeper level.

More than 30 years ago, Hersey and Blanchard (1977) advised us that it was critical to provide greater amounts of structure to newer or less mature teams. Our own experience with hundreds of schools and districts from across the country has also taught us that you cannot "overstructure" your Data Teams, especially in the beginning. More simply put, the better the structure, the better the outcomes. Providing clarity on the expected outcomes, norms, processes for carrying out the work, time lines, roles, and responsibilities plays an important role in helping people to work differently together.

A recent study by Higgins, et al. (2010) found that superintendents who focused their efforts on addressing the team's structures, processes, and tasks "were significantly more likely to have a positive effect on team member growth and learning" (p. 44). We will provide specific guidance on the team's structures later but want to emphasize here that structures help individuals and teams to function more effectively. (Also see Saunders, et al., 2009, and Gallimore, et al., 2009.)

LEADERSHIP AND CHANGE

We will discuss specific leadership practices in several of the following chapters; however, here we want to provide some basic guidance on leadership. The primary responsibility of leaders is to move the organization toward meeting its goals. Few people believe anymore that this can be done individually; rather, what is required is the development of leaders at all levels of the system. We will discuss the different forms of shared leadership in relation to the district, building, and instructional-based teams in other chapters; however, none of this mitigates the need for leadership on the part of the principal, the central office staff, and the superintendent. Without leadership from them in an ongoing way, it is impossible to develop leadership across the system. Having completed numerous quantitative and qualitative studies on leadership, we feel confident saying that leadership boils down to a balance between **pressure and support**.

Pressure

Nothing in the system will change without pressure. Individuals and the system are perfectly content to continue getting the results that they are getting. Therefore, if you want different results, lead differently. To be an effective leader, you must create a degree of discomfort or some form of dissonance between where the system is now, and where it needs to be as a school or district. Kotter (1996) says that the biggest mistake that people make in leading change is not creating enough of a sense of urgency. The proposed changes must be important enough to individuals personally for them to be motivated enough to change. This is what Fullan (2009a) refers to as a "moral purpose"—something that is personally important enough to a person that it is worth taking the risk to change his practices.

One way to achieve this is to personalize the student achievement data by putting a "face" and name on every data point. Having done this, however, the leader must also provide the right structures to give enough psychological safety so that staff members feel comfortable when they talk about the data. Monitoring, feedback, and data all can create a positive sense of ongoing pressure.

Support

If we are going to push people to change, then we also need to support them in being successful. This includes utilizing traditional approaches to learning like professional development, but it must include much more. If we really want people to change their practices, we must meet them where they are and provide them with individualized support so that they can be successful. Weinbaum and Supovitz (2010), in a three-year longitudinally mixed method study on implementation, found that once we are clear about what practices we want to emphasize, then we "must consider the level of complexity that the change presents to school staff. More complex changes will demand a higher level of both engagement and support" (p. 69).

If the goal is to make continuous improvement, then one of the primary responsibilities of the Data Teams at all levels must be to identify the learning needs of individuals and teams and provide the supports necessary for learning. This is a new and challenging role for most teams. When individuals and teams are making progress, everything is fine. However, when individuals or teams are not making progress, it becomes the responsibility of the teams (at the school and district level) to analyze why and to make recommendations for more effective interventions and supports. We will talk more about this later, but it is important to emphasize that the team structure creates opportunities to examine multiple and deeper perspectives on what is happening and why. The teams also have a more realistic and grounded perspective in terms of recommending specific instructional practices and needed supports, as well as interventions, to continue to move the work forward expeditiously.

The graphic of the yin-yang symbol (Exhibit 1.1) is meant to represent how the potentially opposite or contrary forces of pressure and support can, when kept in balance, support the learning needs of individuals and groups.

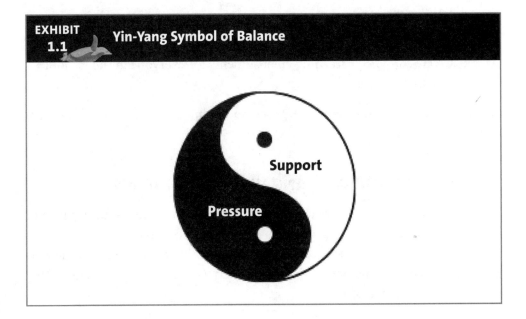

EXHIBIT 1.1   Yin-Yang Symbol of Balance

Support

Pressure

CHAPTER 2

The Improvement Framework

In this chapter we will outline the improvement framework. If you review the six components that follow you will see that, on the surface, this framework is relatively simple to comprehend. Having said that, in this case, "simple does not mean easy." Deep implementation is never easy. Part of this is due to the fact that we try to do too many things and stretch ourselves too thin. Another reason is that we usually don't monitor our implementation well, which means that we don't really know how well we are doing. Finally, we are also challenged by the fact that we typically don't improve systemically; as a result, we tend to repeat many of the same mistakes. Following through on the six components of the framework helps to address each of these concerns.

1. Use data well and in an ongoing way.
2. Limit the number of goals and strategies, and focus on them.
3. Develop shared instructional practices.
4. Implement deeply.
5. Monitor, provide feedback, and give support.
6. Create supportive learning environments for everyone in the "school system."

While we will discuss the components separately, in practice they are interactive and often iterative.

USE DATA WELL AND IN AN ONGOING WAY

Data are used to identify district, building, and classroom needs and to measure implementation and ongoing progress in addressing these needs.

While the first component of the framework is "data use," this is somewhat misleading, because data are used continuously within each component of the framework. Data are used to:

1. Establish goals (for the district, buildings, and classrooms).

2. Guide discussions about instructional practices.

3. Monitor the implementation and effectiveness of the Data Teams (district, building, and instructional).

4. Monitor the implementation of the strategies.

5. Evaluate the impact of the strategies on students.

6. Provide feedback to staff on the strategies and teams and the impact they are having on students.

7. Assess the effectiveness of the professional development supports.

What should be evident here is that data are used at every level of the system to provide feedback on the effectiveness of our efforts. The collection of data is feedback to the system; it is not a mechanism for punishment. If you are making progress, keep doing what you're doing. If you are not making progress, you need to do something different and then evaluate how effective that is. Within each component of the framework you will see the use of data. The kinds of data that are collected and analyzed are often new to schools and districts, however. For example, monitoring data should be collected that tells you whether or not you are implementing the instructional strategies and the teams well. These data then inform the Building Data Teams (BDTs) and District Data Teams (DDTs) as to their progress and next steps.

District-Level Data Use

The District Data Team (DDT) should begin the process with a comprehensive review of district-level data, including the state assessment results, other summative data (like quarterly benchmark assessments), and any ongoing formative assessment data. The District Data Team (DDT) should also review other data, including attendance, retention, suspension, expulsion, pass rates for specific grades and courses, and so on.

The purpose in reviewing this data is to gain consensus regarding the most important areas for improvement. There should be no more than three goals for improvement and not more than one or two strategies per goal.

The section "Limit the Number of Goals and Strategies and Focus on Them" discusses focused goals and strategies; however, once the District Data Team (DDT) has identified its goals and strategies, data collection and analysis move toward focusing on measuring both the degree of implementation and the effectiveness of the instructional strategies on student performance. Therefore, two primary ongoing data sources need to be monitored and reviewed by the District Data Team (DDT): implementation data and effectiveness data.

Implementation Data

Implementation data should be collected by each Building Data Team (BDT) concerning two things: how well the strategies are being implemented by staff in the buildings and how well the Instructional Data Teams (IDTs) are being implemented. Depending on the specific instructional strategies chosen, this data might be collected from rubrics, lesson plan reviews, walk-throughs, and other sources. Multiple questions need to be addressed by both the District Data Team (DDT) and the Building Data Team (BDT), such as:

1. How will we know if the instructional strategies and the Instructional Data Team (IDT) are being implemented effectively and appropriately?
2. What data should we collect?
3. How do we collect this data?
4. How often should we collect this data?
5. How do we report this data back to the staff?

These questions will instigate new and important discussions for both the District Data Team (DDT) and the Building Data Team (BDT), because these teams are responsible for collecting, analyzing, and interpreting the data. It is also important that these data be "benchmarked" over time by individuals on the District Data Team (DDT). By this we mean that District Data Team (DDT) members should visit schools and conduct collegial walk-throughs and observations with members of the Building Data Team (BDT) to increase the reliability of the data being collected.

Effectiveness Data

The District Data Team (DDT) should review any ongoing student performance data that the district collects, such as quarterly benchmark assessments and any other regularly administered assessments. Ongoing data from the buildings should also be reviewed. The question that the District Data Team (DDT) needs to be able to answer is, "Are students making progress as a result of the strategies being used?"

Building-Level Data Use

Buildings have data like the state assessment and other district benchmark data, but in addition they usually have some formative data. For example, most elementary buildings collect data on reading (like DIBELS). Other schools may have other formative assessments that they have either developed or purchased. The Building Data Team (BDT) needs to decide what kinds of student performance data to review and how often these data need to be reviewed to ensure that all students are making progress. The Instructional Data Teams (IDTs) should be facilitating the development and administration of their own common formative assessments as a part of the process. In both cases, the Building Data Team (BDT) should have ongoing student performance data to review.

Implementation Data

The Building Data Team (BDT) will also need to collect data on the level of implementation of the specific instructional practices chosen by either Building Data Team (BDT) members or by the District Data Team (DDT). We will discuss this in greater detail in Chapter 8; however, it is important to understand that the Building Data Team (BDT) will need to decide how to collect, analyze, and report data on how well the instructional strategies and Instructional Data Teams (IDTs) are being implemented. This requires some form of data-collection tools or strategies, like lesson plan reviews or the development of observation checklists or rubrics that define the level and quality of the practices that can be observed, collected, analyzed, and reported.

Effectiveness Data

Effectiveness data are data that help to inform the team as to whether the strategies or practices are having a positive effect on student performance. For both the Building Data Team (BDT) and the Instructional Data Team (IDT), these data should include the common formative assessments being used. They could also include a review of student work samples. The effects of using research-based instructional practices should be evident first in the quality of student work being produced. While you should not be naïve in assuming that any single strategy will have a significant impact on the outcome of your state assessment, it is reasonable to expect that the combination of continuously learning new, more powerful instructional practices, while simultaneously working in Instructional Data Teams (IDTs) that examine and strengthen ongoing instruction, should result in raising student outcomes on these assessments.

The important point to be made here is that both the Building Data Team (BDT) and the Instructional Data Team (IDT) should use ongoing data to assess both student progress and the progress of their implementation.

Instructional Data Teams

Reeves (2002) says that, when used effectively, a data-driven decision-making process acts as a continuous process that requires data gathering, analysis, and correction to decision making on a regular basis. Instructional Data Teams (IDTs) use a formal, six-step process at every collaboration meeting (this process will be discussed in depth in Chapter 5):

1. Collect and chart the data (Treasure Hunt).

2. Analyze performance data and prioritize needs.

3. Set, review, and revise incremental SMART goals.

4. Identify instructional strategies.

5. Determine Results Indicators.

6. Monitor strategies and use of the process.

Cause Data and Effect Data

Instructional Data Teams (IDTs) use two types of data—cause and effect. Teams examine "effect data," also known as student learning data (Bernhardt, 1998). The student performance data are generated by a common formative assessment, which is administered within a data cycle. Teams also collect "cause data," which represent specific adult actions (use of the strategies) used to impact results. Strategies could encompass instruction, programs, processes, and organization. Think back to the Introduction, when we discussed antecedents. White (2005) reports that the cause data are what determine which strategies to replicate, subtract, and refine. Data Teams collect cause data as a result of their use of instructional strategies, processes, and resources, and they use cause data to make midcourse corrections.

LIMIT THE NUMBER OF GOALS AND STRATEGIES AND FOCUS ON THEM

Having reviewed hundreds of building- and district-level improvement plans at The Leadership and Learning Center, we can say without a doubt that the majority of improvement plans have too many goals and strategies (see Reeves, 2010). Consequently, the efforts of staff are spread across so many initiatives that they are rarely implemented effectively, nor do they achieve the intended outcomes. If we want and expect staff to be more effective at making continuous progress toward the improvement goals that we set for the school and districts, we "need a small number of clear priorities to execute well" (Bossidy and Charan, 2002, p. 69).

District Data Teams—Goals and Strategies

Based on a review of the district-level data, the District Data Team (DDT) needs to identify a limited number of focused goals that are stable over an extended period of time (not a year or two, but five to 10 years). A number of prominent researchers have concluded that district improvement plans are too complex and have too many goals, strategies, and activities. Instead, these plans should contain a limited number of focused goals and strategies (Fullan, 2009a; Reeves, 2009; Levin, 2009). Reeves (2009) concludes that "complex organizations that create meaningful change in a short period of time are not weighed down by voluminous strategic plans; they have absolute clarity about a very few things that must be done immediately" (p. 243).

Patterson, et al. (2008) found that "a few behaviors can drive a lot of change … enormous influence comes from focusing on just a few *vital behaviors*" (p. 23, emphasis in original). He and his colleagues went on to recommend, "You should pay special attention to a handful of *high leverage* behaviors" (p. 28).

While the idea of limiting the number of goals or priorities has innate appeal, districts all too often feel compelled for a variety of reasons to say that they are involved in every "new" reform initiative. This is the "Christmas tree" model where the district has every new shiny program or bauble (but not much progress). Reeves (2010) refers to this as "institutional multitasking." He says that while this approach has some "seductive appeal," the benefits are neither efficiency nor effectiveness; instead, they provide the appearance of importance and the illusion of indispensability (p. 64). While this frenetic pace may impress some folks (maybe even some politically important people), trying to "do everything" only results in doing nothing well.

We have worked in high-need districts and it is easy to see that there are many needs and multiple demands. These multiple demands often create a "priority paradox" (Reeves, 2010) where, politically, districts feel compelled to create multiple initiatives to try to address as many of these issues as possible. Based on our work with hundreds of districts, we can say confidently that this approach is misguided. As we all know, having 10 priorities is equivalent to having no priorities at all. This is why we recommend having a limited number of focused goals and strategies that are stable over time. Elmore (2004) and Fullan (2006) both found that there is not a lack of innovations in districts and buildings, but rather a proliferation of too many initiatives. Fullan (2008b) cites Eric Abrahamson when he says that "Initiativitis," or "repetitive change syndrome," is the tendency to launch an endless stream of disconnected initiatives that no one could possibly manage (p. 1). We know from Bossidy's work (2002) that effective leaders are leaders who execute, and they execute well because they have fewer, clearer, more focused priorities to which they pay close attention.

Based on the research and our own successful experiences, we recommend that districts establish a limited number of two or three focused goals that are stable over an extended period of time. Based on these goals, specific improvement strategies can be selected by either the district or the building. We have seen this be effective in both cases. The key, however, is to have a limited number of focused goals and strategies that are kept stable over time.

Let us be clear here—the outcome of this focused work is not to develop a plan! There are too many plans already. The goal is to use ongoing planning, implementation, and monitoring. Reeves (2006) found: "When it comes to planning documents, ugly beats pretty, provided that ugly is not a reflection of wanton messiness, but rather thoughtful consideration of the continuous updates and modifications that make planning documents correspond to reality. Most importantly, ugly surpasses pretty when it comes to the most important variable of all: student achievement" (p. 63). His point is, the functionality of the plan is what matters. Plans that are not used and modified in an ongoing way don't matter. Plans that are well used and modified over time are much more effective. "Exquisitely formatted planning documents are worse than a waste of time" (Reeves, 2006, p. ix). The "prettiness of the plan ... is inversely (or should we say perversely?) related to student achievement" (p. 64).

The purpose of the plan is to provide a clear focus for the district and to communicate the importance of that focus to everyone in the district. Once the District Data Team (DDT) has determined the appropriate goals for the district, these goals should be adopted by the board and then remain stable over an extended period of time. Districts like Norfolk, Virginia, which has made continuous improvement for close to ten years, have maintained the same district goals for that extended period of time. The goals have remained stable, but the strategies have changed and improved as they have moved along.

Building Data Teams—Goals and Strategies

Once the goals are established by the district, these goals should be used to set specific targets for each Building Data Team (BDT) to address. The strategies should be limited to two things: implementation of research-based instructional practices and the effective use of Instructional Data Teams (IDTs).

The choice of which specific instructional strategies to learn can be made by either the District Data Team (DDT) or the Building Data Team (BDT). While the goals remain stable over time, the instructional strategies can change based on the progress made in implementing strategies. However, there again is a caution to not choose too many strategies. As we will discuss soon, the level of implementation matters greatly. (For a review of which components really make a difference in district plans, see Reeves, 2010.)

Instructional Data Teams—Goals and Strategies

Effective Instructional Data Teams (IDTs) align their areas of instructional or curricular focus to those of the Building Data Team (BDT). Stephen Covey (2004) tells us to focus on the "wildly important." He defines a wildly important goal or area of focus as one that will have serious consequences if we fail to achieve it. Instructional Data Teams (IDTs) focus on curricular areas that have leverage and promote 21st-century learning, that will help close the achievement gap with subgroup populations, and that provide necessary skills for success in school and life. Instructional Data Teams (IDTs) focus as they generally select one curricular area at a time, teach, and assess, making midcourse corrections until all students have developed a depth of understanding and results are achieved.

DEVELOP SHARED INSTRUCTIONAL PRACTICES

There is clear consensus in the research regarding the need for districts to focus on both student achievement and the quality of instructional practices, including using specific forms of instruction (Togneri and Anderson, 2003; Simmons, 2006; Supovitz, 2006; Leithwood and Jantzi, 2008; MacIver and Farley-Ripple, 2008; Marzano and Waters, 2009; Fullan, 2010). While the idea that district and school staff should focus on the quality of instruction is not new, what *is* new is the increased involvement that leaders at every level of the system should play in that instructional improvement.

For some time now we have been saying that principals need to be instructional leaders, but we now know that the same is true for superintendents and central office staff. They all need to be more focused on improving academic achievement by improving instruction. Unfortunately, involvement in instructional improvement is still much too rare for administrators at every level.

Instructional Leadership

How do leaders expect to improve instruction if instruction is not their most important priority? While most leaders would agree that it is important for teachers to focus on the success of each child, it should be equally important for principals, central office staff, and superintendents to have the success of every student and every staff member in every building be their highest priority.

According to Elmore (2004, p. 66), "The purpose of leadership is the improvement of instructional practices and performance regardless of role." To begin this work, we first need to agree on what we mean by high-quality instruction. Without some consensus on what is meant by high-quality instruction, every building and every teacher is left to define this on his own. This variability in understanding across the district continues to perpetuate the same variability in performance.

The single most important influence on student learning is the quality of teaching, yet most schools and districts have not defined what they mean by "good" or "effective" teaching (Simmons, 2006). If you believe that this is true, then you need to work collectively to define and agree upon what high-quality instruction looks like in the classroom and then work toward the consistent implementation of these practices across every school in the district. While there are a number of ways to achieve this kind of consensus, the two specific approaches detailed in the next sections are particularly helpful.

Regardless of whether the instructional strategies are chosen by the district or the building, it is beneficial to go through one the following approaches at both levels, because it is important for staff at both levels to develop a consensus regarding what effective instructional practices look like and how they can effectively use these practices in classrooms. To do this, both District Data Team (DDT) and Building Data Team (BDT) members need to participate in a more formal process of classroom observations. (For a more comprehensive description on instructional rounds, see City, et al., 2009.)

Develop Your Own List of Effective Practices

In Chapters 3 and 4 we will also discuss the importance of developing a collective understanding of high-quality instructional practices, because this shared understanding forms the foundation for all of the district and building improvement work. Without this consensus on instruction, it is difficult to make consistent progress. Jackson (2009) makes the point: "Moving beyond merely analyzing and interpreting readily available data requires purposeful inquiry. An interesting starting point can be to create knowledge about existing good practices . . . and to use this affirmative inquiry as a model for transfer and wider learning" (p. 284).

The following exercise can take some time depending on your schedule, but it is time well spent. We recommend that both the District Data Teams (DDTs) and Building Data Teams (BDTs) go through this process and then reach consensus on their findings.

As a Data Team (at the district and building levels):

1. Review building-level performance data from across the district or across the school and identify consistently high-performing teachers at various grade levels, subjects, or courses. High-performing teachers should include those teachers whose students have exceeded expectations for at least three consecutive years on state assessment measures.

2. Members of the District Data Teams (DDTs) should pair with members of the Building Data Team (BDT) to conduct at least three observations for each teacher during different times of the day. When Data Team members are in these classrooms, they should look for and record what they see in terms of high-quality instructional practices. The observers should be as detailed as possible in terms of describing what the teacher was doing and what students were doing.

3. Data Team members should work individually and then collectively to develop a "draft" list of high-quality instructional practices or "look-fors."

4. Team members should then organize the practices into an instructional framework of how and when the instructional practices might be used for student learning. While there are many ways to organize instruction, the outcome of this step is to provide clarity on when the particular practices might be used appropriately. For example, Gagne (1985) outlines the following steps:
   - Have an opening activity to gain attention.
   - Present the learning objectives.
   - Activate prior knowledge.

- Present and model the content.
- Guide an independent practice.
- Provide feedback.
- Assess the performance.
- Retain and transfer the practice.

(You may also want to review the instructional design questions by Marzano [2007] as a way to think about organizing the instructional practices.)

5. The District Data Team (DDT) should then work with Building Data Teams (BDTs) and other staff members to gain consensus on a robust description of these practices and the framework.

6. The District Data Team (DDT) should then refine and share this list with the Building Data Teams (BDTs), and then with the entire staff of the district, to reach agreement on the strategies and the framework. They then select specific strategies to work on for improvement across the school and district.

7. After agreement has been reached on working on specific strategies, the Data Team should develop specific rubrics that describe in detail what the practices look like when they are being implemented well. The rubrics are then used to collect data when walk-throughs are being conducted and to provide feedback to staff.

Review the Research on Effective Instruction

The second strategy is to work with the District Data Team (DDT) and the Building Data Teams (BDTs) to review the research on effective instruction. The research literature on effective teaching and learning is particularly robust. While we are not able to provide a comprehensive review of the research on instruction here, we will highlight some of this research. It is important to realize that we are now at a point in time that we know quite a bit about high-quality instruction. In the following we highlight some of the important research findings.

The Role of the Principal

Wahlstrom and Louis (2008) examined the need for instructional leadership at the building level and the importance of the principal being *actively* involved in the instructional work. While the principal plays an essential role in instructional improvement, they also found that the principal must develop opportunities for shared leadership. A specific finding from the research of Wahlstrom and Louis

(2008) was that "when instructional leadership is shared among the teachers *and* with the principal, the influence of the combined efforts on the quality of pedagogy is significant" (p. 483). In their meta-analytic study, Marzano, Waters, and McNulty (2005) made a similar finding that principals need to develop shared or distributed leadership in order to effectively implement the needed improvement practices.

Instructional Data Teams and the Role of the Teacher

In their analysis, Wahlstrom and Louis (2008) also identify powerful teaching practices that have a significant impact on student learning. These teaching practices include:

1. Providing attention to specific learning goals with plenty of choices and interesting things to think about.

2. Presenting material in small steps that are linked with opportunities for guided practice.

3. Presenting information in multiple different ways.

4. Involving students in problem solving through the active exploration of new ideas and applications to real-life problems.

5. Using questions to help assess students' understanding.

6. Assisting students in developing cognitive and metacognitive strategies that enable them to perform higher-level operations independently.

While not meant to be an exhaustive review, this list can provide some helpful guidance as to what powerful teaching and learning look like in a classroom. For our purposes, it provides a starting point for discussions and consensus regarding what powerful teaching looks like. Effective teachers are clear about the learning outcomes, present the information in different ways, break the learning into small steps with guided practice, and provide opportunities for real-life applications, problem solving, metacognition, and reflection.

It is particularly interesting to notice the overlap between the research of Wahlstrom and Louis (2008) and the research cited in the list that follows. Take a minute to compare the previous list with the following list. What similarities or differences do you notice?

Darling-Hammond and Bransford (eds., 2005) cite the work of Pamala Carter (n.d.), who identified a set of common practices among highly effective teachers and found that "although teachers differed in their ages, backgrounds, and personalities, the researchers found that the teachers 'offered a remarkably similar picture' of effective teaching (including):

- Expectations for the students were clearly stated and exemplars of previous years' assignments were shown to students as models of what to produce.

- Student work could be found everywhere; inside the classroom, out the door, and down the hall.

- The teachers did not stand still and lecture; they covered every part of the room and monitored every activity that took place.

- Multiple small-group activities were often found, while the traditional arrangement of desks and rows was practically nonexistent.

- There were high levels of "instructional discourse": students were encouraged to ask questions, discuss ideas, and comment on statements made by teachers and other students.

- The organization of the room and the lessons was clearly evident. Materials were easily accessible when needed, and no class time was wasted from lack of preparation" (p. 6).

Darling-Hammond and her colleagues (2008) state, "There are at least three fundamental and well-established principles of learning that are important for teaching:

1. Students come to the classroom with prior knowledge that must be addressed if teaching is to be effective . . .

2. Students need to organize and use knowledge conceptually if they're to apply it beyond the classroom . . . [and]

3. Students learn more effectively if they understand how they learn and how to manage their own learning" (pp. 3–4).

They go on to identify what they call "principles of learning for effective teaching." They found that "looking across domains, studies consistently find that highly effective teachers support the process of meaningful learning by:

- Creating *ambitious and meaningful tasks* that reflect how knowledge is used in the field.

- Engaging students in *active learning*, so that they apply and test what they know.

- Drawing *connections to students' prior knowledge* and experience.

- Diagnosing student understanding in order to *scaffold the learning process* step-by-step.

- *Assessing student learning continuously* in adapting teaching to student needs.

- Providing clear *standards*, constant *feedback*, and opportunities for work.

• Encouraging *strategic and metacognitive thinking* so that students can learn to evaluate and guide their own learning" (p. 5; emphasis in original text).

They bridge a division in educational ideology by concluding that "the combination of appropriately timed direct instruction with the results of inquiry has been found to be superior to either approach alone" (p. 17).

In her most recent book, Darling-Hammond (2010) goes on to say that the key elements in effective schools include the careful scaffolding of learning of complex skills, "the conscious use of multiple instructional strategies, well-managed small-group work, real-world connections, and community service and internships" (pp. 254–255), as well as flexible supports (in-class and beyond-class supports), additional time (before and after school), and peer tutoring. Hopefully as you review these different researchers and findings, you will begin to see an emerging consensus on what powerful teaching and learning look like.

While Darling-Hammond (2010) referenced the use of multiple instructional strategies, Marzano, et al. (2005) chose to examine the research on specific, effective instructional strategies to see which strategies had the greatest impact on student learning. He and his colleagues identified nine categories of effective instructional strategies, each of which was correlated with increases in student achievement. The strategies that they identified included:

1. Identifying similarities and differences.

2. Summarizing the note taking.

3. Reinforcing efforts and providing recognition.

4. Providing homework and practice.

5. Providing nonlinguistic representation.

6. Providing cooperative learning.

7. Setting objectives and providing feedback.

8. Generating and testing hypotheses.

9. Providing questions, cues, and advance organizers.

This analysis is different from the other research studies referenced earlier. In this meta-analytic study, Marzano, et al. (2005) were not examining broader teaching and learning practices but rather were determining the quantitative effect sizes for individual teaching strategies (or percentage gain in student performance).

In *The Art and Science of Teaching,* Marzano (2007) cautioned about using the nine instructional strategies randomly, or only based on the magnitude of their effects. Instead, he recommended that educators think about the strategies in terms of lesson or, even better, unit design. In this book he identified specific instructional design questions that both teachers and administrators should consider in lesson or unit development. These questions include:

1. "What will I do to establish and communicate learning goals, who tracks student progress, and celebrate success?

2. What will I do to help students effectively interact with new knowledge?

3. What will I do to help students practice and deepen their understanding of new knowledge?

4. What will I do to help students generate and test hypotheses about new knowledge?

5. What will I do to engage students?

6. What will I do to establish and maintain classroom rules and procedures?

7. What will I do to recognize and acknowledge adherence and lack of adherence to classroom rules and procedures?

8. What will I do to establish and maintain effective relationships with students?

9. What will I do to communicate high expectations for all students?

10. What will I do to develop effective lessons organized into a coherent unit?" (p. 7)

Marzano (2007) went on to identify (1) specific action steps associated with each of these instructional design questions and (2) how to appropriately think about using the nine instructional strategies.

In 2008 Marzano and his colleagues identified a set of critical commitments that they concluded must also be addressed if we are serious about improving schools. One of these commitments is to ensure that there is effective teaching in every classroom. In this commitment he recommends that districts and schools systematically explore and develop a model or language of instruction based on action research regarding specific instructional strategies. This is similar to the process that was identified earlier in this chapter. He then recommends using the instructional strategies along with the instructional design questions listed earlier. He also recommends that teachers observe other "master teachers" appropriately using the instructional strategies. He further says there is the need to monitor the use of the strategies on a school-wide and district-wide basis, including the provision of feedback to all teachers on the effectiveness of their instruction.

Most recently, Marzano (2009) has cautioned: "Focusing on any single set of categories exclusively is a serious mistake. . . . The entire constellation of strategies is necessary for a complete view of effective teaching" (p. 31). He goes on to say, however, "While beginning with a narrow focus is legitimate, a school or districts must expand the breadth of its discussion of effective teaching" (p. 32). He then identifies nine comprehensive strategies that relate to effective teaching, including:

Content

1. Lessons involving new content.

2. Lessons involving practicing and deepening content that has been previously addressed.

3. Lessons involving cognitively complex tasks (generating and testing hypotheses).

Routine activities

4. Communicating learning goals, tracking student progress, and celebrating success.

5. Establishing and maintaining classroom rules and procedures.

Behaviors enacted on the spot

6. Engaging students.

7. Recognizing adherence and lack of adherence to classroom rules and procedures.

8. Maintaining effective relationships with students.

9. Communicating high expectations (2009).

Within these nine comprehensive strategies, Marzano identifies 41 specific teaching strategies that should also be addressed. Part of the reason why Marzano presents this information is to address his concern regarding the misuse of the nine instructional strategies and to help educators think more deeply about the use and misuse of strategies.

In a similar vein, Hattie (2009) conducted a 15-year review of more than 800 meta-analyses and 52,637 studies, resulting in the most comprehensive review of research-based practices to date. In exploring teaching practices and their influence on achievement, he concluded, "The biggest effect on student learning occurs when teachers become learners of their own teaching, and when students become their own teachers" (p. 22). This finding certainly supports the concept of schools as learning organizations, beginning with the student.

Hattie also found that schools that doubled their performance followed a similar set of strategies that included:

1. Goal setting.

2. Analyzing student data.

3. Using formative assessments.

4. Collectively reviewing evidence on good instruction.

5. Using time more productively.

This finding supports the concept of schools creating the structures, expectations, and opportunities for collective learning using data and Data Teams. Hattie also found that effective schools had leaders who provided strong instructional leadership (p. 257). Effective instructional leaders focused on improving instruction through the use of common formative assessments in Instructional Data Teams (IDTs) that set high goals, evaluated good instruction, individualized instruction, and used time more productively. Hattie might have been describing the Data Teams process when he said that what matters "is attending to personalizing the learning, getting greater precision about how students are progressing in this learning, and ensuring professional learning of the teachers about how and when to provide different or more effective strategies for teaching and learning" (p. 245).

In synthesizing the research on teaching and learning, Hattie (2009) identified seven specific criteria that were associated with student learning:

1. Paying deliberate attention to learning intentions and success criteria.

2. Setting challenging tasks.

3. Providing multiple opportunities for deliberate practice.

4. Knowing when the teacher and students are successful in obtaining these goals.

5. Understanding the critical role of teaching appropriate learning strategies.

6. Planning and talking about teaching.

7. Ensuring that teachers constantly seek feedback information as to the success of their teaching on student learning (p. 36).

This list has many similarities to the other lists; however, it includes specific actions that teachers should take to inform their teaching, like seeking feedback from students and talking and planning with their peers about their own teaching.

In his book, Hattie (2009) also presents data from multiple studies that explore the specific contributions to achievement that come from students, schools, and teachers and from specific teaching approaches and practices. For example, he explores how the magnitude of the effects differ from teaching approaches such as reciprocal teaching, direct instruction, inquiry-based teaching, problem solving and problem-based teaching, and cooperative learning. In summarizing all of this work, Hattie identifies "six signposts of excellence" in education:

1. "Teachers are among the most powerful influences in learning.

2. Teachers need to be directive, influential, caring, and actively engaged in the passion of teaching and learning.

3. Teachers need to be aware of what each and every student is thinking and knowing, to construct meaning and meaningful experiences ... to provide meaningfully appropriate feedback.

4. Teachers need to know their learning intentions and the success criteria of their lessons, know how well they are attaining these criteria for all students, and know where to go next.

5. Teachers need to move from the single idea to multiple ideas ... and to extend these ideas.

6. School leaders and teachers need to create school, staffroom, and classroom environments where error is welcomed as a learning opportunity" (pp. 238–239).

This last signpost focuses on creating learning organizations where teachers and other leaders are actively engaged in exploring how to make teaching more powerful and learning more personal for everyone in the building.

While this is only a small overview of the research on teaching and learning, we recommend that you explore this information more deeply and use the results of your work to initiate discussions with members of both the District Data Team (DDT) and Building Data Team (BDT). Beginning with these research reviews, the teams can develop their own "language of instruction" grounded in their own observations and the research. From here, they can develop an instructional framework that is shared across schools and the district.

IMPLEMENT DEEPLY

Doug Reeves (2006, 2008, and 2010) has presented data on the critical importance of deep implementation for a number of years. Most recently he found that "*half-hearted implementation was actually worse than minimal or no implementation*" (2010, p. 36; emphasis added). He found in his studies that unless you can implement to the 90 percent level, you should not expect to get the outcomes that are promised in the research. It is probably fair to say that most schools and districts currently do not meet this 90 percent implementation standard. In the next section on monitoring, feedback, and support, we'll discuss how to determine the level of implementation you do have, but here we want to talk about the need for implementing more deeply.

In Chapter 1 we identified and discussed the problem of follow-though in most schools and districts, where there is a large gap between how well we *think* our initiatives are being implemented versus how well our initiatives really *are* being implemented. In Chapter 1 we recommended using both top–down and bottom–up approaches, focusing on a few important strategies that can make a significant difference to student achievement. By focusing everyone on learning to effectively use more powerful instructional practices (top–down) and implementing collaborative Data Teams (bottom–up), we can focus our learning on implementing a few things well and reduce the implementation gap.

Deeper implementation is tied to a number of important factors, including:

1. Focusing on the shared learning of a few important things (instructional practices and Data Teams).

2. Increasing the effectiveness of ongoing professional development, including opportunities for ongoing practice and coaching, and the use of the instructional practices by opinion leaders.

3. Providing a high level of monitoring, feedback, and support (discussed in the next major section, "Monitor, Provide Feedback, and Give Support").

Focusing on a Few Important Things

As stated in Chapter 1, the biggest challenge we face is our inability to implement well. To address this concern, we recommend focusing on two approaches for improvement:

1. Learning and deeply implementing specific effective instructional practices.

2. Using Data Teams at each level of the system.

These two approaches become the primary focus for the improvement work.

Increasing the Effectiveness of Professional Development and Learning

If we are going to implement deeply, we need to seriously rethink the way that adults learn. Traditional forms of professional development (e.g., "sit and get" lectures, conferences, book studies) have proved to be inadequate to achieve the deep implementation that is required.

Darling-Hammond and her colleagues (2009) cautioned that current forms of professional development do not provide either the intensity or duration necessary to have a noticeable impact on instruction or student learning. They went on to say that in order for professional development to have a positive impact on improving student learning, the primary focus of professional development efforts must be on instruction, and it needs to provide for active and sustained teacher learning. The most effective ways to focus our improvements on instruction (i.e., learning, applying, and practicing powerful instructional practices) is through the development of teacher-based, or Instructional, Data Teams (IDTs). In addition to the Instructional Data Teams (IDTs), Darling-Hammond, et al. (2009) also found that teachers needed time to learn and to practice new instructional strategies. Reeves (2010) made a similar finding that "deliberate practice is the key to improved performance" (p. 66).

Learning to use more effective teaching practices requires learning in Instructional Data Teams (IDTs), undergoing traditional professional development, and then having the opportunity for extensive practice. It may also require having opportunities for demonstration, coaching, and observation for some learners. If everyone is going to learn to use the strategy well, we need to learn how to provide the appropriate intensity of learning supports for everyone to be effective. This focus on instructional strategies with opportunities for practice, along with the Instructional Data Team (IDTs), becomes the learning agenda for the building and district.

Providing Monitoring, Feedback, and Support

Opinion Leaders

As stated in Chapter 1, it is also extremely beneficial to gain the support of opinion leaders in the building. Having opinion leaders use and model the strategies facilitates the more rapid acceptance and use of the strategies across the building.

Having the District Data Team (DDT) and the Building Data Team (BDT) focus on how well individuals are using the strategies and how effectively they are functioning in the Instructional Data Team (IDTs) provides the teams with both positive and negative examples of implementation from which the teams can learn. Who is experiencing success? Why? What can we learn from this? Who's not being successful? Why? What other supports need to be provided? What can we learn from this? If we can't implement even a few small things deeply and well, then there is little chance that we will be able to implement larger or more complex strategies. By starting with small, focused strategies, we can learn more about how to strengthen our supports for implementation.

Short-Term Wins

In Chapter 1 we identified some strategies to assist in closing the implementation gap. Reeves (2009) also recommends creating short-term wins. People need to be able to see positive outcomes as a result of their work in a relatively short period of time. Kotter (1996) identifies several reasons why short-term wins have an effect on the outcomes. He found that short-term wins reduce skepticism, build momentum, and provide motivation to staff members that their efforts are worth it. Short-term wins also provide concrete feedback about the effectiveness of the chosen strategies. Reeves (2009) also found that using formative assessments were an especially important way to demonstrate ongoing progress.

Identify and Recognize Effective Practices Publicly

Another strategy Reeves determined is to continually identify and recognize the effective practices publicly. He found that an important part of monitoring is collecting and providing feedback on the effective use of the practices to staff. Another method he recommended is collecting and posting data that link the use of the practices to student outcomes. These data should be collected and analyzed by both the Building Data Team (BDT) and the District Data Team (DDT). Another way to recognize effective practices is to provide opportunities for classroom observations and collegial walk-throughs so that staff can see practices being implemented well or, in some cases, not so well. These collegial walk-throughs and observations build a shared understanding of how well we are doing in our implementation efforts and build a commitment to better follow through on everyone's part.

Part of the learning process for both the Building Data Team (BDT) and the District Data Team (DDT) is to identify other supports that may be needed to help people implement more deeply. Both teams need to be able to answer the question of "what supports were most effective in supporting our implementation?"

Monitoring, feedback, and support are covered more extensively in the following section.

MONITOR, PROVIDE FEEDBACK, AND GIVE SUPPORT

For the past several years, Reeves (2006, 2010) has presented data on the importance of monitoring. For Reeves, monitoring means focusing on the "adult actions"; i.e., are the adults following through on their implementation of the practices? He found that districts and schools that scored high in monitoring, evaluation, and inquiry had gains that were two to five times greater than schools and districts that scored lower on these dimensions. In his studies, "monitoring" meant that there was the frequent (at least monthly) analysis by the teams of:

1. The use of specific teaching strategies.

2. Formative student performance data.

3. The use of leadership practices that supported the implementation.

As stated earlier, the single biggest gap that we see in schools and districts is the lack of monitoring and feedback. Because in most cases we don't collect data on our implementation effectiveness, we don't really know how well we are implementing. Therefore, it is extremely difficult for us to know whether or not we are making progress with our implementation. All too often we are quick to judge that something didn't work, when the reality was, we never really implemented the practice deeply or well.

The process of monitoring requires that we have some way of collecting data on the level and quality of our implementation. Schools and districts need to be able to answer the question of how well we are implementing both the instructional strategies and the Data Teams process. Both the District Data Team (DDT) and the Building Data Team (BDT) need to develop specific tools or rubrics to collect data on the level of implementation of these two approaches. Remember, however, that the primary purpose of monitoring is to provide feedback to the staff on how well they are implementing. Fullan (2008a) warns us that negative monitoring does not work. It is important to understand that the purpose of monitoring is not to punish people for their lack of follow-through, but rather to collect and analyze the data to provide feedback and to assess how well our implementation strategies (e.g., training, coaching, modeling) are working.

Monitoring should help us determine where our implementation is being successful and where we need more support. The challenge for the Building Data Team (BDT) and District Data Team (DDT) is to interpret the data and decide which specific supports have been effective or ineffective and which strategies to try now in order to move the work forward. Again, these data become an important barometer in terms of our "reciprocal accountability." By this, we mean that if individuals or teams are struggling with their implementation, can they, and do they, seek support and suggestions from other sources? Each person and each team is responsible for the success of one another. If the grade-level, department, or course teams are not being successful, what actions has the Building Data Team (BDT) taken to support them? If the Building Data Team (BDT) needs help, what support has the District Data Team (DDT) provided? We will discuss this issue of support more in Chapter 4, but it is critical to understand that individuals and teams need differential kinds and levels of support if they are going to really implement new practices well.

CREATE SUPPORTIVE LEARNING ENVIRONMENTS FOR ALL EDUCATORS

Twenty years ago, Peter Senge (1990) brought the concept of learning organizations into the mainstream. He proposed that a learning organization is a group of people working together to collectively enhance their capacities to create results that matter to them. He outlined five disciplines as a part of learning organizations; the one that is most important for our purposes here is "team learning."

It seems somewhat ironic that educators would need to consciously work to become learning organizations; isn't that what schools are supposed to be? However, the reality is that most classrooms, schools, and districts don't learn well collectively. By and large, teaching is still an isolated profession. While there are clearly many successful teams in many districts, "there is no tradition or organization that supports carefully supervised learning of this kind" in most schools and districts (Levin, 2008, pp. 80–81).

Elmore (2004) makes the point that improving instruction requires continuous and collective learning on the part of every person in the district. He challenges all of us when he states, "The existing institutional structure of public education does one thing very well: it creates a normative environment that values idiosyncratic, isolated, and individualistic learning at the expense of collective learning. The existing system does not value continuous learning as a collective good and does not make this learning the individual and social responsibility of every member of the system. *Leaders must create environments* in which individuals expect to have their personal ideas and practices subjected to the scrutiny of their colleagues. Privacy of practice produces isolation; isolation is the enemy of improvement" (p. 67; emphasis added).

Leaders play an especially important role in personally leading and demonstrating changes in norms, expectations, and structures that cause people to think and carry out their work in different and more reflective ways. The key to effective change, however, is the ability of leaders to model this learning themselves. Supovitz (2006) found that district leaders play a critical role here. He states, "The *district's capacity to promote and support ambitious instruction hinges on the leader's abilities both to learn themselves and help others to learn new ideas.* In other words, leaders' beliefs about learning predicated the way they conceived of and structured learning opportunities within their own organizations" (pp. 9–10; emphasis added). If we hope to really improve the quality of instruction and educational outcomes for students, leaders must be willing to publicly learn themselves and also to put structures and processes in place that encourage and set expectations for others to learn.

The question of how to change district and school environments to create these kinds of learning environments is addressed through the specific components of the framework discussed in this chapter. By working collectively and collaboratively in teams at all levels of the system to learn from using data, focusing goals and strategies, improving instruction, identifying the successes and challenges of implementation, and monitoring and providing feedback, District Data Teams (DDTs), Building Data Teams (BDTs), and Instructional Data Teams (IDTs) can develop a deeper sense of how to facilitate learning at every level. As Fullan (2008a) says, "Learning is the work" of the teams and the district, or, put another way, Data Teams at each level of the system create the structures whereby "organizational learning is the engine of sustainability" (Supovitz, 2006, p. 160).

Developing teams that are responsible to each other creates a more robust accountability system where each level of the system is responsible for the success of the other levels. Darling-Hammond (2010) sees this shift in accountability as a new paradigm for both schools and districts. "In this new paradigm the design of the school district office should also evolve from a set of silos that rarely interact with one another to a team structure. . . . This means they must continuously evaluate how schools are doing, seeking to learn from successful schools and to support improvement in struggling schools by ensuring that these schools secure strong leadership and excellent teachers, and are supported in adopting successful program strategies. Districts will need to become learning organizations themselves—developing their capacity to investigate and learn from innovation in order to leverage productive strategies and develop their capacity to support successful change" (p. 271).

A similar paradigm shift must occur simultaneously at the building and classroom levels through the establishment of Building Data Teams (BDTs) and Instructional Data Teams (IDTs) that also learn from their own work. The Building Data Team (BDT) should review the ongoing progress of every student in the building, the effectiveness of the instructional strategies being used by teachers, and the effectiveness of each of the Instructional Data Teams (IDTs). If teams are making observable progress, the Building Data Team (BDT) should learn from this and share this learning with other teams in the school. If other teams are not making progress, the Building Data Team (BDT) should intervene and provide differential supports. If the strategies being used by Instructional Data Teams (IDTs) are not effective, then the Building Data Team (BDT) must take similar action. This may involve providing more supports to individual teachers or to Instructional Data Teams (IDTs), or developing tiered interventions for specific students or groups of students. If the Building Data Team (BDT) is not being successful in its efforts, then it must solicit the support of the District Data Team (DDT). Each team is responsible for the success of one another. This may require additional professional development, coaching, or direct leadership by the principal or central office staff.

The bottom line is, all of the teams and team members must take the responsibility to act if students are not making progress. When individual students are not making progress, teachers and the Instructional Data Teams (IDTs) need to try something else. When Instructional Data Teams (IDTs) are not making progress, the Building Data Team (BDT) must intervene to improve their progress. If a building is not making progress, then the District Data Team (DDT) needs to intervene with supports or interventions.

In all of these cases there is a "reciprocal accountability" (Elmore, 2004) between the teams. Each team is responsible for the success of the other teams. It is not okay for one team to let another team not make progress on improvement. Multiple studies have shown that using Data Teams to distribute leadership throughout the systems develops leadership at all levels and improves instruction and student achievement (Chrispeels and Gonzales, 2009). The likelihood of significantly improving classroom practices is limited if we cannot develop broader leadership capacity across each school and the district.

Using powerful teaching strategies and the use of Instructional Data Teams (IDTs) can be a powerful agent of change, but only if the individuals and the teams can learn and make continuous progress. As we have seen, many of the approaches that we have traditionally used for professional development have had a limited impact on teacher practice and therefore on student performance. If teachers can't learn more powerful instructional practices as a result of the team structures, then the teams serve no valuable purpose. If the Building Data Team (BDT) can't assess which strategies or which teams are improving student learning, or which specific supports are needed for individual teachers or teams, then they aren't learning, and everyone continues to make limited progress. If the District Data Team (DDT) can't learn from schools and classrooms what is working, and why, then it can't provide appropriate supports, and the likelihood of replicating or sustaining growth across the district is very limited. If this work is reduced to just carrying out tasks (effective practices and Data Teams), then improvement will be limited. This work gains its power by collecting formative data and feedback from all levels of the system. Just like in classrooms, formative assessment is only formative if it informs the learning.

Schools and districts that make continuous progress create systems, structures, and supports where there is an active inquiry process and follow-up actions that are grounded in data, analysis, reflection, and learning. Reeves (2006) found that schools that were higher in their degree of "inquiry" performed three times higher than their counterparts. He concluded, "If you believe that adults make a difference in student achievement, you are right. If you believe that adults are helpless bystanders while demographic characteristics work their inexorable will on the academic lives of students, you are right" (p. 72). The defining difference is whether the adults take personal responsibility for student achievement. The development of Data Teams at each level of the system supports the development of personal responsibility paired with collective accountability.

SECTION TWO

Data Teams

Leadership as a Team Sport

Section Two of the book is focused on the development of teams at every level of the system (classroom, school, and district). This section highlights the importance of leadership development through shared inquiry grounded in data.

Chapter 3 outlines the research on what we know about effective districts. It highlights the critical role and functions of the superintendent as the leader of instructional improvement in the district. This chapter identifies three critical functions that the superintendent must provide to lead improvement in the district. It also identifies what effective districts do to improve student academic outcomes, identifies the role of the District Data Team (DDT), outlines the membership and purpose of the team, and provides key questions for the District Data Team (DDT) to address. Finally this chapter outlines the primary strategies for improvement.

Chapter 4 focuses on the Building Data Teams (BDT). This chapter reviews the most current findings on principal leadership and student achievement. The reader will note that the single largest effect of principal leadership on student achievement is attained by having the principal be the lead learner in the school. This is achieved by focusing the entire school on learning more powerful instructional practices and systematically using data in teacher-based Instructional Data Teams (IDTs). This chapter identifies the importance of the building-level Data Team \and provides guidance on the membership, purposes, and functions of the team. Finally this chapter identifies the primary strategies to successfully make progress.

Chapter 5 identifies the critical importance of the teacher-based Instructional Data Teams (IDTs). It highlights the necessity of collaboration and outlines the specific six steps of the Data Teams process. The most recent research on the effective use of teacher-based teams identified the need for teachers to follow specific protocols if they were going to be successful in raising student achievement (see Galimore, et al., 2009, and Saunders, et al., 2009). Given these findings, it is particularly important for principals and Building Data Teams (BDTs) to provide leadership in the form of structures, supports, monitoring, and feedback to their teacher-based Instructional Data Teams (IDTs) if they want them to be successful in raising student performance.

Chapter 5 focuses on Instructional Data Teams (IDTs). This chapter is geared toward the implementation of teacher teams and is focused on administrators and teachers leading this process at their schools. This chapter will provide an overview of the Instructional Data Team. You will learn the purpose and structure of the teams, as well as the data-driven process Data Teams use: inquiry, collecting and charting the data, analysis of student performance, incremental SMART goals, determination of strategies, crafting of results indicators, and monitoring the process.

CHAPTER 3

District Data Teams (DDTs)

DISTRICT LEADERSHIP

It was only a few years ago that we had conflicting studies regarding whether principal or superintendent leadership positively impacted student achievement. More recently, however, studies have shown that building and district leaders *can* have a beneficial impact on student achievement. Studies have gone on to say that without effective leadership at the building and district levels, progress is unlikely (Robinson, et al., 2008; Leithwood, et al., 2007; Leithwood and Jantzi, 2008; MacIver and Farley-Ripple, 2008; Marzano, Waters, and McNulty, 2005; Marzano and Waters, 2009). Another important finding is that there cannot be sustained improvement at the building level without effective district leadership. Ultimately, there must be effective leadership at every level to achieve sustainable progress.

Although there are multiple examples of individual schools that have made significant progress, these schools do not usually continue to make progress unless there is leadership at the district level to support their efforts. MacIver and Farley-Ripple (2008) highlighted this connection when they stated that "researchers (have) pointed out candidly that despite the evidence of effective schools here and there, most teachers and principals do not exhibit the characteristics of those found in 'effective schools' and there is a need for leadership at the district level to help assure that more individual schools become more effective schools" (p. 8).

We will discuss the importance of principal leadership in Chapter 6, but here we will focus on the critical role of the superintendent and central office. Let's begin with a discussion of the role of the superintendent in district improvement.

Superintendent's Role in District Improvement

Marzano and Waters (2009) found that the correlation between superintendent leadership and student achievement was statistically significant and associated with almost 10 percentile point gains. Interestingly, the overall effect size for superintendents was similar to the effect size for principals (see Marzano, Waters, and McNulty, 2005). This is surprising given the direct impact that principals have on teachers and therefore on students. It is heartening, however, to know that superintendents can provide specific leadership actions that can influence student outcomes. As we will see, the most important of these actions is a concerted focus on improving instruction in the classroom.

It is common for superintendents to be the public spokespersons for their districts. As the designated leader, it is also common to have superintendents publicly acknowledge the need for high expectations for achievement. Less often, however, do we see superintendents actively involved in the district improvement process, and it is even more rare to see them actively involved in the improvement of instruction. As it turns out, this can be a fatal flaw for superintendents whose districts are not making measurable gains in student performance, or not making adequate yearly progress (AYP).

In order to improve outcomes in every school, district leaders—and especially superintendents—need to play a more active role in instructional improvement. Supovitz (2006) advises that "school district leaders who wish to improve the performance of all students within their system must make a concerted effort to employ the central lever that is in their power to improve student learning—the fulcrum of instructional improvement" (p. 1). He goes on to caution that "district leaders who do not articulate a coherent vision of good instruction will cede instructional leadership either to individual schools or outside providers, or some unmanageable combination of the two. The consequences of this will be uniform mediocrity at worst and far-flung variation at best" (p. 27). Superintendents need to realize that neither site-based management nor outside programs and consultants will be sufficient for their districts to make significant improvements in student achievement. Instead, they must personally and directly exercise leadership in the area of instructional improvement. We now have a number of studies that have emphasized the critical importance of superintendent leadership in this area (Honig, et al., 2010; Simmons, 2006; MacIver and Farley-Ripple, 2008; Marzano and Waters, 2009; Supovitz, 2006).

Next, we will recommend three specific ways in which superintendents should involve themselves in the district's instructional improvement work. It is the superintendent's direct involvement in this work that makes this everyone's focus and highest priority and that conveys to all of the staff in the district the importance of learning about and improving instruction.

Three Important Ways that Superintendents Need to Be Involved in Instructional Improvement

While certainly some superintendents are actively involved in instructional improvements, this is not the norm. The amount of time that most superintendents spend in classrooms, or working with others on instructional issues, is still minimal in most districts. If instructional improvement is important for the district, it must be important work for the superintendent. But the questions still are, how and where do superintendents best focus their attention on instruction?

In our intensive work with districts over the last three years, we have documented the three most important areas that superintendents have used to effectively lead the work of instructional improvement in their districts. We will outline these areas separately in the sections that follow; however, all of these involve leading the instructional improvement work through the District Data Team (DDT). The superintendent, with the District Data Team (DDT), works to make the District Data Team (DDT) become the "guiding coalition" (Kotter, 1996) that implements, monitors, evaluates, learns, supports, and reports on the district's progress regarding instructional improvement. This guiding coalition (including the superintendent) leads the continuous improvement work of the district.

These three critical areas for superintendent involvement in instruction are:

1. Establish and maintain a focus on high-quality instruction.

2. Develop and distribute leadership widely across the district through the use of instructionally focused Data Teams.

3. Develop and model a district-wide system of inquiry, learning, and follow-through with Data Teams at every level (District Data Team [DDT], Building Data Team [BDT], and Instructional Data Team [IDT]).

Establish and Maintain a Focus on High-Quality Instruction

Because high-quality instruction is the most important work, the superintendent must become the lead learner on instruction. This does not mean that the superintendent is the expert on instruction, but rather that the superintendent sets the example that everyone has more to learn *about* instruction. The superintendent must emphasize the expectations that "everyone involved is working on their practice, (and) everyone is obliged to be knowledgeable about the common task of instructional improvement" (City, et al., 2009, pp. 4–5). The message, beginning with the superintendent, is that everyone is responsible for learning more about instruction and must follow through on that learning.

Superintendents, working with the District Data Team (DDT), accomplish this in two important ways. They *develop a shared language and understanding of high-quality instruction,* and they *learn more deeply how these more powerful instructional practices can be used effectively* by carefully observing classroom practices with others on the District Data Team (DDT) and Building Data Team (BDT).

Develop a Shared Language and Understanding of High-Quality Instruction

The first step of this work involves clearly articulating a vision of high-quality instruction for the district. This should include a vision of high expectations, high performance, and high-quality instruction. This vision clearly elucidates what high-quality instruction looks like for teachers and students (Simmons, 2006; Togneri and Anderson, 2003; Supovitz, 2006; Leithwood and Jantzi, 2008; MacIver and Farley-Ripple, 2008; Marzano and Waters, 2009; Fullan, 2010). Raising expectations for increased performance and higher-quality instruction starts with the superintendent. The constant and clear refrain from the superintendent must be "better outcomes through better teaching."

Having a clear, shared understanding of what we mean by "high-quality instruction" is an important starting point for district improvement. Without this shared understanding, it is difficult to share or achieve a goal of improved instruction. Some researchers (City, et al., 2009) recommend that this shared understanding of effective instruction should emerge inductively out of the process of classroom observations. While there certainly is merit in this inductive kind of approach, we have found greater benefit from a more direct approach that grounds the learning of District Data Team (DDT) and Building Data Team (BDT) members in observing the most effective teachers and then developing a consensus around these effective practices.

In Chapter 6 we outline a process for the superintendent and District Data Team (DDT) to identify high-quality instructional practices. The purpose of this process is for individuals and Data Teams to gain a shared understanding and agreement across the district of what high-quality instruction looks like. One thing that we have learned from working with districts from across the country is that we cannot assume that everyone shares a common understanding of what we mean by "high-quality instruction." We agree with City, et al. (2009) that "most educators are working, for better or worse, at, or very near, the limit of their existing knowledge and skill" (p. 8). Therefore, it is probably more realistic to work from the assumption that we do *not* share a common understanding or definition of high-quality instruction but that we can *learn* what good instruction looks like together.

The superintendent and members of the District Data Team (DDT) should conduct this activity together. Undertaking this learning collectively conveys to everyone involved that "we all have more to learn about instruction." Having the superintendent and the District Data Team (DDT) spend time in classrooms observing instruction publicly conveys a commitment to high-quality instruction and also sets an expectation for similar learning to be carried out by the Building Data Team (BDT) and the teacher-based Instructional Data Teams (IDTs). Is important for the superintendent to demonstrate and articulate that ongoing learning about instruction is the most powerful form of professional development. Carrying this work out as a District Data Team (DDT) also conveys that team learning at *all* levels should be the primary way in which we learn and apply new practices.

Once the District Data Team (DDT) has developed a draft list of effective instructional practices, this list needs to be developed into a draft of an instructional framework. It is important for the District Data Team (DDT) to publicly share this work and begin to use the "draft" descriptions of effective practices. However, the list of effective practices and the instructional framework should be refined over time based on the District Data Team's classroom observations and understanding and on feedback from others in the district.

Learn More Deeply How Instructional Practices Can Be Used Appropriately in the Classroom

The superintendent and members of the District Data Team (DDT) should conduct both walk-throughs and classroom observations on a regular basis. The purposes of these two activities are different. Walk-throughs are usually used for monitoring and to gather and report data on the implementation of specific instructional practices that the district or building has selected as important for everyone to learn and use appropriately. The purposes of classroom observations, however, are to learn more about instruction, convey the importance of learning more about instruction, and to provide feedback to the Building Data Team (BDT) about the overall quality of instruction in the building. Classroom observations are meant to provide continued learning opportunities for the superintendent and the District Data Team (DDT).

During these observations, the District Data Team (DDT) should divide into smaller groups of two to three people and conduct classroom observations for 15 to 20 minutes in a number of classrooms in a specific building. Their observations should focus on the specific areas for improvement identified by the district or for that specific building.

In classrooms, team members record their observations of what teachers are doing and what students are doing. During the debrief, members of the team then share with each other and with members of the Building Data Team (BDT) what they saw teachers and students doing, and they make recommendations to the members of the Building Data Team (BDT) to strengthen their instructional improvement efforts in the building. (For information on a similar process, see City, et al., 2009.)

In the following chapters we will discuss having Building Data Team (BDT) members and teachers from the Instructional Data Team (IDT) also conduct classroom observations and walk-throughs. These efforts are similarly aimed at deepening everyone's understanding of instruction and gaining broader-based consensus on the implementation of our improvement efforts.

Once the superintendent and the District Data Team (DDT) have a draft framework of effective practices and have participated in classroom observations and walk-throughs, District Data Team (DDT) members will conduct additional walk-throughs to monitor and "benchmark" the implementation of the district- and building-level strategies. In order to do this, they will need to develop rubrics that clearly identify what the strategies look like when they are being implemented well.

Develop and Distribute Leadership Widely Across the District through the Use of Instructionally Focused Data Teams

While you can still find leadership books that extol the concept of the single heroic leader, most of the current theory and research cited in books and articles on leadership support the concept of distributed, disbursed, or shared leadership (Kotter, 1996; Collins, 2001; Spillane, 2006). To successfully improve instruction across the entire district, most districts need more instructional leaders with greater capacity to support instructional improvement work in every classroom. While we know from the research that individual leadership on the part of the principal and the superintendent are essential, we also know that to be successful as an organization we need to develop more leadership opportunities, responsibilities, and accountability for the success of each classroom and school in the district. I believe it was Ralph Nader who said that the measure of a good leader is how many leaders they leave behind. Simply put, "Effective leaders create more leaders."

For our purposes, the measure of an effective leader is how many other leaders and leadership opportunities he creates at all levels of the system. Developing opportunities, structures, and systems that support leadership development starts with the superintendents. They accomplish this goal by establishing effective Data Teams at the district, building, and classroom levels. They use the team structure to create leadership opportunities that will develop leadership capacity at each of these levels. "Superintendents need to find ways to extend their sphere of influence beyond the formal positions of power. Building teams that can extend the superintendent's power base by generating effective solutions and implementing them requires a collaborative approach to leadership" (Higgins, et al., 2010, p. 44).

The Use of Data Teams District-Wide

The superintendent's commitment and participation are critical to the success of all Data Teams. Through their own actions, superintendents set the expectations for the teams, model collaborative behaviors, and hold people to the norms, structures, processes, and outcomes that the team establishes.

Because the District Data Team (DDT) should include teachers and administrators who may not interact with the superintendent on a regular basis, it is particularly important for the superintendent to create an atmosphere where everyone can discuss the "brutal facts" with candor and inquiry. We have seen multiple examples where superintendents working with their District Data Teams (DDTs) either open up and deepen the questions and discussions or completely shut down conversations with a single comment.

Multiple perspectives can be extremely helpful when complex issues are being addressed; however, often these critical perspectives are not shared. In our work with District Data Teams (DDTs) we heard over and over again from team members some version of the following comment: "What you (at the central office) think is being done, is not really going on at the building and classroom levels." The discrepancy between "what is" versus "what we think" is often quite large.

Because the district often provides for some level of professional development, district staff members often think that there is greater implementation at the building and classroom levels than there really is. If the goal is to accurately assess the district's progress and make adjustments, then the District Data Team

(DDT) needs an honest assessment of the "brutal facts." The superintendent causes this to happen by publicly acknowledging the facts openly in District Data Team (DDT) meetings, supporting ongoing inquiry into why, and ensuring that the team has the appropriate structures, processes, and facilitation necessary to move the work forward.

Recently, a study by Higgins, et al. (2010) found that "superintendents who coached their teams by focusing on the teams' task processes were significantly more likely to have a positive effect on team member growth and learning" (p. 44). What they are referring to here is that the superintendent must ensure that there is clarity about the tasks that the team is to accomplish (what the specific work is), and about the team structures and processes to accomplish those tasks. They went on to say, "It is critical for superintendents to create a team environment in which team members feel comfortable speaking up and stepping in to help—a 'psychologically safe' team environment" (Higgins, et al., 2010. p. 45).

Superintendents do this in several specific ways. First, they provide expectations for the District Data Team (DDT) in terms of the outcomes of the group's work. Second, they clarify roles and responsibilities of District Data Team (DDT) members. Third, they ensure that structures and processes are in place for the team to be successful. The provision of the right structures, processes, and tasks by the superintendent is critical to the team's success (Higgins, et al., 2010). We have said for some time that it is impossible to overstructure the Data Teams. It is easy, however, to understructure the teams. Structures like norms, agendas, role assignments (process facilitators, timekeepers, devil's advocate, etc.), decision-making structures, minutes, follow-up assignments, and so on, all contribute to the team's success.

Develop a District-Wide System of Inquiry, Learning, and Follow-Through with Data Teams at Every Level (District Data Teams, Building Data Teams, and Instructional Data Teams)

Currently, most districts have limited processes for inquiry. By limited, we mean that their inquiry process is not very deep or well developed. Usually, central office staff members limit their inquiry to outcome data, such as a review of whatever formal data sources they have (e.g., state assessments, benchmark assessments, and any other student assessment data, along with attendance and discipline data). What most districts do not have is an ongoing inquiry process based on multiple perspectives from across the district that looks at adult implementation (or cause data) to know or understand why they are, or are not, making progress. All too often, when schools or the entire district are not making progress, what occurs is tantamount to the "kick the dog" theory, where the superintendent blames the central office staff members, who blame the principals, who blame the teachers, who blame the students and their families.

In a true inquiry process, district and building staff members have the interest and capacity to go deeper and to address the kinds of questions that are identified at the end of this chapter. As inquiry teams (District Data Teams [DDTs], Building Data Teams [BDTs[, Instructional Data Teams [IDTs]), they should be able to assess whether or not they are making progress, and have the capacity, structures, and processes to examine these questions. The teams should know which specific adult actions resulted in the outcomes that they got. The teams should know and understand which supports are necessary and effective in terms of student, teacher, and team learning and also be able to effectively strategize the right next steps.

In reviewing the improvement framework in Chapter 2, we outlined in some detail the importance of both inquiry and learning in making continuous progress. We also highlighted in that chapter the importance of the superintendent personally leading the inquiry and learning work. We cannot overestimate the critical leadership role that the superintendent plays in modeling the leadership behaviors that are positively associated with collaborative inquiry.

Inquiry is a reflective, problem-solving process. Collaborative inquiry is a reflective process for teams to study and act on shared problems. It might be compared to a collective-action research cycle, where data analysis is used to understand the underlying causes of the outcomes; actions to improve performance are proposed, examined, and agreed upon; then the actions are implemented, monitored, and reexamined by the teams.

For the District Data Team (DDT), this involves examining the implementation and effectiveness of the district-level strategies (specific instructional practices and Data Teams). When the buildings and the district *are* making progress, it is the District Data Team's responsibility to analyze what contributed to this success and to assess "can we replicate this?" When the buildings or district *are not* making progress, it is the District Data Team's responsibility to assess whether this is because of a lack of implementation, not the right supports, or other potential causes, and then to make recommendations regarding how to rectify this.

More specific details will be provided in this chapter and in following chapters on the development of the Data Teams at the district, building, and classroom levels. However, it is important that the superintendent set the expectation that there needs to be an active, ongoing inquiry process at every level of the district. The superintendent also needs to communicate the expectation that *all* educational professionals in the district must be willing to examine the effectiveness of the leadership and teaching practices that they are using, and be willing to strengthen or improve them. Moreover, superintendents must ensure that the team processes and structures are in place for the District Data Teams (DDTs), Building Data Teams (BDTs), and Instructional Data Teams (IDTs) to address these expectations.

Most superintendents are involved to varying degrees in the development of district plans, such as strategic plans, accountability plans, or improvement plans. In this case, however, superintendents must demonstrate leadership through their active and ongoing participation in the District Data Team (DDT) and in the follow-through that is required. As the designated leaders of districts, superintendents must articulate this vision, set expectations, and work with the District Data Team (DDT) to develop, implement, monitor, and evaluate the district's focused improvement efforts. They also must ensure that the team structures and processes are in place for the Building Data Teams (BDTs) and the Instructional Data Teams (IDTs). With the District Data Team (DDT), the Building Data Team (BDT), and the Instructional Data Team (IDT), the collaborative inquiry process should be represented as the most effective form of active, ongoing, collaborative professional development. This is what high-quality professional development should be—active, ongoing inquiry based on data, learning, and deep application of that learning.

Central Office Role

Not that long ago there was a limited amount of research on what directly contributed to developing effective school districts. The prevailing belief system had been based on earlier research that seemed to indicate that site-based management was effective (i.e., give schools more autonomy and then let them each figure out what works for them). While districts retained a variety of management functions, such as hiring, budgets, buses, buildings, and centralized assessments, it was believed that the most effective strategy for districts was to get out of the way and let buildings select and implement their own chosen improvement strategies.

MacIver and Farley-Ripple (2008) found that "districts that have sought to promote decentralized decision-making about curriculum have found the need to become more prescriptive . . . decentralization resulted in too much fragmentation in curriculum and instruction" (p. 33). In many districts this resulted in having each building adopt its own approaches to teaching specific content areas.

In some districts this resulted in having as many approaches to teaching reading as there were buildings.

In their meta-analyses, Marzano and Waters (2009) made similar findings and came to the conclusion that the average correlation between site-based management and student achievement was, for all practical purposes, 0.0. Their recommendation was for districts to develop a degree of "defined autonomy," meaning that the superintendent should expect principals and other administrators to lead within the boundaries of the district goals for instruction and achievement (p. 8).

The research findings guide districts toward what may be called "loose–tight" properties. Districts need to tighten their guidance in a number of specific ways (see the list that follows regarding what effective districts do to improve student academic outcomes) that result in closer alignment between the district and the buildings. There are, however, many other areas where the district should provide more flexibility to the buildings. The District Data Team (DDT) should provide clarity and direction in the areas of curriculum, instruction, and assessment, and work with the Building Data Teams (BDTs) on specific implementation strategies. Everyone should be on the same page, giving the same message. "Research (has) show(n) that districts can influence school improvement efforts, (however) weak guidance from knowledgeable central office staff undermines (the) school's use of (that) knowledge" (Mangin, 2007, p. 326). It is not surprising, therefore, that the more recent research has swung toward a more active role for districts. More effective districts take a more active role focused on improving instruction.

MacIver and Farley-Ripple (2008) also found that "central office administrators are crucial in the school improvement process" (p. 8). However, they also found that if district staff members provide conflicting advice to schools, or weak support for the district's initiatives, it impedes the progress of the entire district. The district needs to have a process that develops a broad-based understanding and support for the district's goals and strategies. The Data Teams at the district, school, and instructional levels should be the primary mechanisms to develop this shared understanding of what is needed and how those goals and strategies can be supported.

In reviewing the most recent research, there appears to be fairly strong consensus on what effective districts do to improve student academic outcomes. Many of these findings have been identified by a number of recent researchers (see below), however the recommendations identified are heavily grounded in the work of the work of Leithwood & Jantzi (2008) and an extensive large scale, six year leadership study by Louis, et al. (2010).

1. A focus on student achievement and on the *quality of instructional practices*, including the use of effective research-based instructional practices (Togneri and Anderson, 2003; Simmons, 2006; Supovitz, 2006; Leithwood and Jantzi, 2008; MacIver and Farley-Ripple, 2008; Marzano and Waters, 2009; Fullan, 2010; Harris and Chrispeels, 2009).

2. Development of *instructional leadership* at the district, school, and classroom levels, including training for central office staff, principals, and teachers on high-quality instruction and the leadership of improvement (Togneri and Anderson, 2003; Leithwood and Jantzi, 2008; MacIver and Farley-Ripple, 2008; Fullan, 2010; Harris and Chrispeels, 2009).

3. Training, capacity building, support, and expectations in the *effective use of data* across the district, in decision making, and in assessing student learning and progress. Emphasis on the role of the principal in promoting and participating in the formal and informal use of data (Togneri and Anderson, 2003; Marsh, et al., 2005; Leithwood and Jantzi, 2008; MacIver and Farley-Ripple, 2008; Fullan, 2010; Harris and Chrispeels, 2009; Filbin, 2008; Fullan 2008).

4. *Collaborative goal setting in establishing a limited number of focused, nonnegotiable district goals* for achievement and instruction that are stable over an extended period of time. Creating understanding and support for the district goals from school boards, community partners, and all school staff (Leithwood and Jantzi, 2008; Marzano and Waters, 2009; Fullan, 2010).

5. *Monitoring the implementation of the strategies, evaluating the results, and creating feedback loops* to all staff on progress in achievement and instructional goals (MacIver and Farley-Ripple, 2008; Marzano and Waters, 2009).

6. Ongoing, targeted, and differentiated *professional development*, and the *phasing in of improvement efforts over time* (Leithwood and Jantzi, 2008; Harris and Chrispeels, 2009; Darling-Hammond, et al., 2009).

7. *Distributing leadership* with an emphasis on the development of teams and professional communities (Leithwood and Jantzi, 2008; Harris and Chrispeels, 2009; Hattie, 2009; Darling-Hammond, et al., 2009).

8. *Allocating and aligning resources* to support the goals for achievement and instruction, including district-sponsored professional development

(Togneri and Anderson, 2003; Leithwood and Jantzi, 2008; Marzano and Waters, 2009; MacIver and Farley-Ripple, 2008).

While all of the district conditions are significantly correlated to student achievement, the strongest relationship is with the district's concern for student achievement and the quality of instruction (Leithwood and Jantzi, 2008; MacIver and Farley-Ripple, 2008). The most consistent finding across all of the studies is the importance of the district maintaining a strong focus on improving instruction, while raising standards and achievement (Bottoms and Fry, 2009).

In reviewing this list, what should beome clear is that the research strongly recommends that the primary focus for the district should be on improving instruction. The focus of this instructional improvement should include the two primary strategies (Data Teams at every level; shared learning and application of research-based instructional practices). Too many districts are overly ambitious when it comes to establishing goals and strategies. The research recommends, however, that districts learn by focusing on a few important things (in instruction) and then examining the effectiveness of their implementation. Districts do this by focusing on a limited number of goals and strategies that can be implemented deeply and monitored, and for which feedback can be provided frequently. Districts then tailor support through professional development opportunities like peer observations, coaching, and modeling. Once these strategies are implemented deeply, other instructional practices can be phased in over time.

While there is a need for some traditional professional development in the areas of high-quality instruction and data use, the best way for teachers to learn about instruction is from other teachers; therefore, the primary way to deliver professional development should be through the Instructional Data Teams (IDTs). Professional learning occurs not just in the Instructional Data Teams (IDTs), however, but in all of the Data Teams, including the District Data Teams (DDTs) and the Building Data Teams (BDTs). These teams also become the primary mechanism for distributing leadership across the building and the district.

By following the components of the framework outlined in Chapter 2, the district can reinvent itself into a continuous learning and improvement organization whose primary responsibilities are to improve learning and provide effective supports across the district.

Darling-Hammond (2010) says that district central offices must "create a new paradigm" in which the role of the central office and district must shift:

- "From enforcing procedures to building school capacity.
- From managing compliance to managing improvement.

- From rewarding staff for following orders and 'doing things right' to rewarding staff for getting results by 'doing the right things.'
- From rationing educational opportunities to expand in successful programs.
- From ignoring (and compounding) failure in schools serving the least powerful to reallocating resources to ensure their success" (p. 270).

In working with districts to implement the research recommendations, we have found that the idea of focusing and deepening the work has resonated with many districts. The idea of using data to focus on a limited number of goals and strategies to improve instruction that are implemented deeply and monitored well sounds seductively simple. The good news is that these are all relatively simple ideas; the challenge, however, is that they are not easy to implement well across the district. As Phil Schlechty (2009) has often said, "Simple is not easy."

Darling-Hammond (2010) says: "In this new paradigm the design of the school district office should also evolve from a set of silos that rarely interact with one another to a team structure.... This means they must continuously evaluate how schools are doing, seeking to learn from successful schools and to support improvement in struggling schools.... Districts will need to become learning organizations themselves—developing their capacity to investigate and learn from innovation in order to leverage productive strategies and develop their capacity to support successful change" (p. 271).

While these changes will be challenging to most districts, having the right focus, structures, and processes makes progress possible and more probable. What we discuss next is the District Data Team (DDT) membership, purpose, and structures that are needed to effectively carry out the work.

District Data Team Role

Usually, when talking about district-level teams, we tend to include only representatives from the central office. In this case it is vital that the membership be broader than just the superintendent and the cabinet. It is important when members are being chosen to systematically identify and recruit opinion leaders from across the district. It is also critical that the superintendent be a visible and active player in the District Data Team (DDT).

Membership of the District Data Team

The following individuals should be included in the District Data Team (DDT):

- Superintendent
- School board member
- Central office staff (assistant superintendents or executive directors for instruction [CAO], elementary and secondary schools, student support services, business services, CFO or treasurer, etc.)
- Principals
- Teacher union and opinion leaders from elementary and secondary schools, including content areas, grade levels, specialty teachers, and program areas (special education, Title I, gifted, ELL, etc.)
- Other stakeholders, including parents and business and community opinion leaders

The size and membership of the District Data Team (DDT) are both important to the success of the work. The District Data Team (DDT) should be large enough to adequately represent the district but small enough to function effectively and efficiently. The overall size of the team is dependent on the size of the district; however, the range is typically between seven to 20 people.

Purpose of the District Data Team

The primary goal of the District Data Team (DDT) is "the improvement of instructional practice and performance, regardless of role" (Elmore, 2004, p. 66). The District Data Team (DDT) becomes the "guiding coalition" (Kotter, 1996; Fullan, 2009b) that leads the improvement work of the district forward. The District Data Team (DDT) reviews the district's data, develops the district improvement plan (including goals and strategies), ensures the provision of professional development and other supports, monitors the implementation and effectiveness of the strategies (or lack thereof) in each building, and learns how to replicate and sustain success. This team actively communicates the improvement work of the district between classrooms, buildings, and the district. District Data Team members, including the superintendent, should actively model the use of inquiry and learning in the process. The team members publicly explore what *is* working in the district and why they think that is. They also look at what is *not* working in an attempt to also assess why.

Our experience in working with districts has taught us that most districts cannot answer either of these questions in any detail. We are not used to deeply examining the causes for the outcomes that we are getting (the adult actions), nor are we used to examining why we are getting these outcomes. Initially, it is extremely difficult to have these kinds of open, candid conversations. This can only happen when the process is fully supported and modeled by the superintendent. As one superintendent said recently, "You have to check your ego at the door."

The District Data Team (DDT), the Building Data Team (BDT), and the Instructional Data Teams (IDTs) create multiple opportunities for shared leadership across the system. These teams create an "ever widening circle of leadership" (Barber, 2009).

Key Questions for the District Data Team

The following questions should be used as a starting point for discussions among the District Data Team (DDT) members.

1. How clear are you and the team on the district's need for improvement?

    • How much consensus is there on the need for improvement? Is there a sense of urgency with the staff?

    • Have you made any measureable gains? How do you know?

    • Do you need to? For which subgroups?

    • Do you know which schools and teachers *are* being successful right now? Do you know *why*?

    • Do you know which schools are *not* being successful right now? Do you know *why*?

    • Do you know which students are being successful right now? Do you know why?

2. How clear are all team members on the district goals and strategies for improvement?

    • How confident are you, and other staff, regarding the strategies?

    • How many goals and strategies are there? Do people know what the goals and strategies are? How do you know?

    • How well are the strategies being implemented? How do you know?

    • How do you assess if the strategies are being effective (when they are being implemented)? What data do you collect? How do you collect this? How often? What is done with these results? What actions have you taken? What student work do you look at?

3. What, how, and when do you provide professional development or other supports? Feedback?

  • How do you measure the effectiveness of your professional development? How do you assess if staff are implementing the strategies? How do you know if the strategies are working?

  • How do you know if people need more?

  • What do you do if people need more?

  • What other supports does the district provide? Have they been successful? How do you know?

4. Does the District Data Team (DDT) have a systematic way of learning from the schools and providing ongoing supports?

  • How do you identify and replicate success?

  • How do you reduce or shorten failure?

  • What supports for differentiated professionals are provided (observations, modeling, coaching, etc.)?

When beginning the process, many districts cannot answer these questions completely. We recommend that the District Data Team (DDT) initially review these questions and then follow the framework provided in Chapter 2. (If you have not reviewed Chapter 2, please review that now.) As you work through the framework, you will need to develop structures, strategies, and processes that, if implemented well, will answer each of these questions fully.

Primary Strategies to Successfully Address the Questions

The primary strategies that the District Data Team (DDT) should follow are outlined in detail in Chapter 2. They include:

1. **Use data well.** Use data to identify district-wide needs and to measure ongoing progress.

2. **Develop and adopt focused goals and strategies.**

3. **Implement shared instructional practices.**

4. **Implement deeply.**

5. **Monitor and provide feedback support.**

6. **Learn as individuals, as teams, and as a system (learning organization).**

Unfortunately, there are no shortcuts to systemic improvement. If you hope to be successful as a school, or district, it takes time, collaboration, trust, and follow-through on everyone's part. To date, many improvement efforts have been fragmented and half-hearted in terms of their implementation. The work outlined here is systemic and therefore harder to start successfully, but it becomes easier as you move along and learn to use the processes and tools regularly. When you complete this book, you should have a good understanding of the framework as well as of recommended structures, processes, and tools to help you implement the framework.

CHAPTER 4

Building Data Teams (BDTs)

Prior to 2005, the research on the effects of principal leadership appeared to be mixed in terms of their effect on student achievement (see the meta-analysis by Marzano, Waters, and McNulty, 2005). However, since that time there have been a number of both quantitative and qualitative studies supporting the positive effect that principals have on student achievement. One finding is consistent across all of these studies: "Of all the variables impacting effective schools, the role of the principal as an instructional leader was paramount. They place priority on curriculum and instructional issues" (Smith, 2008, p. 244).

PRINCIPAL LEADERSHIP

A large body of research now associates principal leadership with increases in student achievement when principals focus on improving instruction (Hallinger and Heck, 1996; Mangin, 2007; Marzano, Waters, and McNulty, 2005; Robinson, 2007; Robinson, et al., 2008). Studies have also indicated that principal leadership is second only to classroom teaching as an influence on student learning (Leithwood, et al., 2007). The importance of principal leadership has become even more important in this era of high-stakes testing and accountability.

Given this fact, one would expect that the principal's highest priority would be a focus on improved instruction and student outcomes, but often this is not the case. As Graham (1997) found in a survey of more than 500 principals, they stated that the majority of the their time is spent in "administrivia" (cited in MacIver and Farley-Ripple, 2008, p. 44). This is often driven by numerous demands from the central office to focus on the management of buildings, budgets, and buses, but it is also driven by multiple demands from within the building (discipline, personnel, parents, etc.).

It is no wonder, then, with multiple and often competing demands placed on the principal, that principals have found it difficult to focus on what should be their most important work—instructional improvement. Faced with these many demands, principals struggle to decide where to best spend what little time they do have. Fortunately, there have been several recent meta-analytic studies undertaken to examine which specific principal practices or responsibilities are positively associated with student achievement (see Marzano, Waters, and McNulty, 2005; Robinson, 2007; and Robinson, et al., 2008). The findings from these studies provide some helpful guidance to principals in terms of which specific leadership actions have the greatest positive effect on student achievement.

In the most recent meta-analytic study, Robinson and her colleagues (2008) identify five key principal leadership practices that positively impact student achievement and provide effect sizes for each. Effect size is a statistical concept that measures the strength of the relationship between two variables. In meta-analyses effect sizes play an important role in summarizing findings from different studies into a single analysis or effect size. In the following study the variables studied are principal leadership actions and student achievement.

1. Establish goals and expectations.

2. Strategic resourcing.

3. Planning, coordinating, and evaluating teaching and the curriculum.

4. Promoting and participating in teacher learning and development.

5. Ensuring an orderly and supportive environment (Robinson, 2007; Robinson, et al., 2008).

We discuss these five findings below but also integrate other research findings and recommendations for implementation of these findings.

Establish Goals and Expectations (Effect Size [E.S.]=0.42)

"Clear goals focus attention and effort and enable individuals, groups, and organizations to use feedback to regulate their performance" (Robinson, et al., 2008, p. 661). Having clear improvement goals and specific teaching strategies can have a direct effect on student achievement at the building by focusing staff members on learning specific researched-based strategies and their impact on student learning.

In many schools and districts there continues to be a parade of new initiatives every year. One approach is piled upon another, while none are implemented well, and none are ever formally removed or discarded. Consequently, teachers and principals end up with multiple demands on their time.

The goal-setting process, when done well, helps everyone in the building to focus on those few things that, if done well, matter the most. Principals and building leaders should use the goal-setting process to gain consensus on the need for improvement and then on the specific strategies to achieve that improvement. By focusing on a limited number of strategies (i.e., instructional strategies and Data Teams), everyone should be able to implement these few strategies well and deeply. "Goals provide a sense of purpose and priority in an environment where a multitude of tasks can seem equally important and over- whelming. Clear goals focus attention and effort and enable individuals, groups, and organizations to use feedback to regulate their performance" (Robinson, et al., 2008, p. 661).

"Goal setting works by creating a discrepancy between what is currently hap- pening and some desired future state. When people are committed to a goal, this discrepancy is experienced as constructive discontent that motivates goal- relevant behavior. Goals focus attention and lead to more persistent effort than would otherwise be the case" (Robinson, 2007, p. 11).

Robinson cautions, however, that goals will only have this motivating effect if three conditions are met:

1. *"Teachers ... need to feel they have the capacity* to meet the goal from either their current resources or from the expertise and support they will receive while pursuing the goal.

2. *People need to be committed to goals,* and this requires that they understand and value them. As long as this is the case, it does not matter whether or not they participate in the actual setting of the goals.

3. *Specific rather than vague goals are required* because specificity makes it possible to judge progress and thus adjust one's performance. Self- regulation is impossible if the goal and therefore, progress towards it, is unclear" (Robinson, 2007, p. 11; emphasis added).

These three conditions provide leaders with some direct guidance on how to effectively engage staff in the improvement efforts. To address the issue of capac- ity building, staff members need to believe that they can successfully accomplish the tasks that are set out for them. It helps significantly, then, to have a limited number of focused goals and strategies so that staff members believe they will be able to implement them successfully.

Staff members also need to experience some early success with their imple- mentation. We want people to make a direct connection between the actions they take and improved outcomes for students, which they should be able to see. It is important that the improvement strategies are powerful and focused enough so that people can see the impact of the strategies in a relatively short period of time. School leaders don't just set the direction, however; they also communicate and emphasize the importance of implementing and monitoring the strategies deeply on a school-wide basis, and they report to the staff on a regular basis on both the level of implementation and the impact on student learning.

It should not be surprising that setting clear goals and strategies helps people to focus their efforts. Nor should it be surprising that when we collectively work toward reaching the goal using more powerful teaching and collaborative teaming, we make progress.

Strategic Resourcing (E.S.=0.31)

This finding was not about the principal or other building leaders securing additional resources; rather, Robinson, et al. (2008) found that student performance was positively impacted when the principal worked to reduce the number of other initiatives in the building and then aligned current resources with the goals and strategies. Numerous other researchers, like Reeves (2006), Elmore (2004), and Fullan (2010), all caution against adopting too many initiatives that detract from the improvement focus on the building and result in "initiative fatigue." Robinson (2007) even cautions that "extra resources can have detrimental effects (because) ... multiple simultaneous initiatives can reduce the coherence of a teaching program" (p. 13).

One of the primary responsibilities of principals and other building leaders is to help staff maintain a focus on the improvement strategies. There are always new projects, programs, grants, or other "shiny baubles" to distract people from the hard work of improving instruction in the classroom. It is the principal's role to limit these distractions and to align resources behind the focused goals and strategies.

Because the largest single resource in any building is the teaching staff, keeping staff focused on the improvement strategies is the most effective use of resources. In implementing the strategies, however, there are several resource issues that will need the attention of the principal and Building Data Team (BDT), including:

• The provision of professional development on the specific instructional practices chosen for improvement, including opportunities for practice, observations, modeling, coaching, and so on.

• Restructuring the school schedule to provide time for the Instructional Data Teams (IDTs) to meet and plan.

• Training and facilitation in the Data Teams process.

We know that using Data Teams can be highly effective (Darling-Hammond, 2010; Gallimore, et al., 2009), but to be effective, there must be training in the process, regularly scheduled time to meet, "predictable, consistent settings," a focus on instruction and student learning, and processes and tools like protocols to effectively carry out the work (Saunders, et al., 2009).

Planning, Coordinating, and Evaluating Teaching and the Curriculum (E.S.=0.42)

This finding refers to the active oversight and coordination of the instructional program in the school. Effective building leaders are actively involved in the instructional process, including having ongoing discussions of instruction, observing classrooms and providing feedback, ensuring that staff members use ongoing assessment results, actively monitoring student progress, and working actively to strengthen instructional practices in classrooms.

Robinson, et al. (2008) found that "leaders in higher performing schools are distinguished from their counterparts in otherwise similar lower performing schools by their personal involvement in planning, coordinating, and evaluating teaching and teachers." Four interrelated subdimensions are involved in this leadership dimension:

"*First*, teachers in higher performing schools report that their leaders are actively involved in *collegial discussion of instructional matters, including how instruction impacts student achievement* (Heck, et al., 1991).

"Second, the leadership of higher performing schools is distinguished by its active oversight and coordination of the instructional program. *School leaders and staff work together to review and improve teaching*—an idea captured by that of *shared instructional leadership* (Heck, et al., 1990; Heck, et al., 1991; Marks and Printy, 2003).

"*Third*, the degree of *leader involvement in classroom observation and subsequent feedback* was also associated with higher performing schools. Teachers in such schools reported that their leaders set and adhered to clear performance standards for teaching (Andrews and Soder, 1987;

Bamberg and Andrews, 2004) and made regular classroom observations that helped them improve their teaching (Bamberg and Andrews, 2004; Heck, et al., 1990).

"*Fourth,* there was greater emphasis in higher performing schools on ensuring that *staff systematically monitored student progress* (Heck, et al., 1990) and that test results were used for the purpose of program improvement" (Robinson, et al., 2008, p. 662; emphasis added).

The Building Data Team (BDT) and the Instructional Data Team (IDT) are where specific discussions of curriculum, instruction, and assessment should occur. Both of these teams should actively monitor the progress of students and examine where and why students are struggling. The discussions in the teams should focus on teaching and student learning and should include the following:

- Using data to identify common learning needs of students.
- Analyzing student work.
- Identifying research-based or promising instructional practices to use collectively.
- Constructing common lessons and units.
- Implementing these lessons and units collectively in the classroom.
- Collaboratively designing, using, and scoring common formative assessments (see Saunders, et al., 2009).

In addition, the principal and Building Data Team (BDT) should actively monitor and provide feedback on the use of, and the effect of, the shared instructional strategies. They do this through collegial walk-throughs, classroom observations, and feedback to staff, and followed up by reinforcing expectations for staff follow-through.

Promoting and Participating in Teacher Learning and Development (E.S.=0.84)

Of all of the findings in this meta-analytic study, the following one had the largest effect size. "This is a large effect and provides some empirical support for calls to school leaders to be actively involved with their teachers as the 'leading learners' of their school" (Robinson, et al., 2008, p. 663). These researchers go on to point out that professional development involves more than principals just arranging for staff to learn. "This leadership dimension is described as *both promoting and participating* because more is involved than just supporting or sponsoring other staff in their learning. The leader participates in the learning as leader, learner, or both.... The principal is also more likely to be seen by staff as a source of instructional advice, which suggests that they are both more accessible and more knowledgeable about instructional matters than their counterparts in otherwise similar lower achieving schools" (Robinson, et al., 2008, p. 663; emphasis added). The principal must be the lead learner of the school and the teams.

When applied to our two strategies (instructional strategies and Data Teams), this means that the principal must actively and deeply engage in the learning and leading of both of these strategies. Principals will need to know (or learn) what the strategies look like when they are being implemented well. They will need to know how to use data well and how to facilitate the Data Teams process with the Instructional Data Team (IDTs).

Principals also need to have a deeper understanding about what powerful professional development looks like and how to provide professional development opportunities that result in actually changing classroom practices. A number of prominent researchers have been examining the connection between changing classroom practices and professional development.

Robinson (2007) identified a number of characteristics that principals need to focus on that were associated with effective professional development, including:

- "Providing extended time and using it effectively.

- Ensuring teachers were engaged in the learning.

- Challenging problematic discourses, especially around low expectations for students.

- *Providing opportunities to participate in a professional community that was focused on the teaching-achievement relationship.*

- *Involving school leaders who supported the learning by setting and monitoring targets and developing the leadership of others"* (Robinson, 2007, p. 17; emphasis added).

There are two very critical points to be made here:

1. Principals must both lead, and be a part of, the professional learning in their school.

2. Principals need to ensure the development of effective Instructional Data Teams (IDTs) and ensure that teachers are actively engaged in the process, are challenging low expectations, and are following up in their classrooms with more effective practices.

This finding directly supports the work of both the Building Data Team (BDT) and the Instructional Data Team (IDT) and the principal's direct involvement in leading this work.

In his large-scale meta-analysis Hattie, (2009) made similar findings regarding the responsibilities of the principal and what worked in professional development. He found that professional development was most effective when:

1. *Teacher learning occurred over an extended period of time.*

2. *Teachers deepened their knowledge and extended their skills* in ways that directly improved student outcomes.

3. *The professional development examined the direct effect that teaching had on student learning, and involved challenging discussions about student learning.*

4. The professional development provided opportunities for *teachers to talk to other teachers* about teaching.

5. Principals supported these opportunities to learn.

6. Schools used external experts (pp. 120–122).

In their analysis, Joyce and Showers (2002) identified four levels of professional development in school, the percentage gain that occurred in knowledge and skills, and the percentage gain that occurred in transfer to the classroom:

• **Studying** the theory produced a 10 percent gain in knowledge, a 5 percent gain in skills, and a 0 percent transfer to the classroom.

• **Demonstration** of the skill produced a 30 percent gain in knowledge, a 20 percent gain in skills, and a 0 percent transfer to the classroom.

• **Practicing** the skill produced a 60 percent gain in knowledge, a 60 percent gain in skills, but still only a 5 percent transfer to the classroom.

• The most effective was pure **coaching**, which produced a 95 percent gain in knowledge, a 95 percent gain in skills, and a 95 percent transference to the classroom.

Joyce and Showers (2002) also found that in order for a moderately complex model of teaching to be implemented, 20 to 25 trials would be required in the classroom over an extended period of time.

When reviewing these findings, what should become clear is that professional development needs to look and be very different from the way it is now in most schools and districts. Professional development must be focused on examining the teaching–achievement relationship and on developing knowledge and skill of how we might teach differently using more powerful teaching strategies. It must also provide opportunities to discuss and challenge low expectations, and for practice, modeling, and coaching on what is being learned.

We have been saying for quite some time now that the time spent by teachers learning and practicing effective strategies, and the time spent in their collaborative teams, should be thought of as professional development. Because this time is specifically focused on improving the quality of instruction, it can be the most effective form of professional development.

The core idea from all of this research is that schools need to become learning organizations. This involves developing an ongoing, school-wide sense of inquiry for both student and staff learning. In Chapter 2 we discussed the expectation that if any of the Instructional Data Team (IDTs) are not making progress, it is the responsibility of the principal and Building Data Team (BDT) to intervene, clarify expectations, and provide for facilitation or other supports to move the team forward. If individual teachers are not following through on implementing the strategies that their team chose, the principal or Building Data Team (BDT) needs to intervene. This is the idea of shared leadership and shared accountability. Similarly, if the building is not making progress, then the District Data Team (DDT) needs to intervene and provide direction and support to staff in the building. When we say that "we are all involved in improving instruction," it means that we share reciprocal responsibility to each other in order to make progress at every level of the system.

Ensuring an Orderly and Supportive Environment (E.S.=0.27)

This finding involves "creating an environment for both staff and students that makes it possible for important academic and social goals to be achieved" (Robinson, et al., 2008, p. 664). This includes having clear codes for conduct or discipline, minimal interruptions of teaching time, and safe and orderly environments. Teachers in higher-performing schools attribute these outcomes to better leadership on the part of the principal. When the researchers examined the relationship between principal leadership and school order, safety, and a supportive environment at a deeper level, they found that "there was a strong statistical link between improvements in relational trust and gains in academic productivity" (Robinson, 2007, p. 19). What the researchers meant by this was that there is a direct relationship between safety, order, supportive environments, and trust in the school. When principals help to create supportive, trusting environments, safety, order, and student achievement improve.

This concept of "relational trust" includes four components: social respect or civil regard; *competence*; personal regard or caring; and *integrity, or doing what you say* (see Bryk and Schneider, 2002; Tschannen-Moran, 2004). While the research suggests that it is possible to develop respect and caring in individuals, it is difficult to develop these kinds of dispositional characteristics. Many of us have heard stories about dogmatic and heavy-handed leaders who have made progress in a school or district, but the reality is that progress is usually short-lived. People do respond to fear and punishment, but they don't learn well under these conditions, and the improvements then don't last. So it may be that principals or other leaders who do not have the ability to demonstrate respect and caring for the people with whom they work should not be in leadership positions.

While it is difficult to develop competencies like respect and trust, it is reasonable to expect that all principals can and should develop competence in the area of instruction. While no one expects principals to be the source of all knowledge on instruction, it is very reasonable to expect that they, like everyone else, must be willing to actively and publicly learn about instruction. Principals can't just say that "instruction is important" and not follow through without sacrificing their own integrity. Hord and Sommers (2008) caution that teachers watch to see if principals who talk about instruction really spend their time on instruction and in classrooms. Jorgenson and Peal (2008) found that teachers lost respect for their principals if they weren't in their classrooms. While teachers understand that principals have many other responsibilities, they also felt that there was no excuse for principals not spending more time in the classroom. Principals need to focus more of their time on their most important responsibility—instruction. This, in turn, builds trust and respect in schools.

> *In schools where trust levels increased over a three year period, teachers reported a greater willingness to try new things, a greater sense of responsibility for their students, more outreach to parents, and stronger professional community involving more shared work, more conversations about teaching and learning and a stronger collective focus on student learning.* Increased relational trust produced more coordinated, mutually supportive and more effective efforts to engage students in learning. With increased trust comes more and better quality cooperation, more social support and a stronger sense of mutual obligation, binding together the efforts

of teachers, principals and parents.... *The relationship between trust and trends in student achievement were apparent even with rigorous control of student and community background variables.* (Robinson, 2007, pp. 20–21; emphasis added)

It is evident from these findings that the principal plays a key role in the development of relational trust, improved cooperation and collaboration among staff, and improved outcomes for students by focusing on what matters most—instruction.

While we will talk more about the implications of these findings, it is interesting to note that the highest effect size was achieved when principals *participated in and facilitated teacher learning and development.* Robinson, et al. (2008) make the point that principals are not just ensuring that their staff members receive professional development, but that principals are actively leading the instructional improvement work and learning from it. Even when they were controlling for students' backgrounds, the researchers found that when principals and other school leaders are actively involved in teacher learning and development, it results in higher student outcomes. This finding has major ramifications for the principal's role with both the Building Data Team (BDT) and the Instructional Data Teams (IDTs).

Robinson, et al. (2008) goes on to say that "leaders who are perceived as sources of instructional advice gain greater respect from their staff and hence have greater influence over how they teach" (pp. 663–664). Conversely, there was no increase in school performance when teachers identified the principal as a close friend or as a participant in discussions. To make a difference in their schools' performance, principals must play a more active and direct role in instructional improvement.

Robinson and her colleagues also made another important finding regarding principal leadership. They found that the impact of instructional leadership (E.S.=0.42) was almost four times more powerful than transformational leadership (E.S.=0.11). This is not to say that transformational leadership (or collaborative leadership) is not important, but rather, when it comes to increasing student performance, instructional leadership is paramount.

Several recent studies have examined the specific components that make up instructional leadership and have made new and important findings with ramifications for principals. What these studies have found is that, *in terms of student achievement, the most important part of instructional leadership is the principal's use of data.* Fullan (2008b) found that "the effect sizes of principals promoting and participating directly with teachers in the formal and informal learning of the use of data to influence appropriate instructional activities were more than twice as powerful as any other leadership dimension" (p. 31). Part of the reason for this is that "active engagement with data of various kinds seems to prompt a more focused, improvement oriented conversation" (Portin, et al., 2009, p. 62). When principals provide strong instructional leadership around the use and application of data to inform instructional effectiveness, it results in higher levels of teacher collective efficacy and greater gains in student achievement (Filbin, 2008).

These findings have important implications for where and how principals spend their time and highlight the importance of the principal's role in both the Building Data Team (BDT) and the Instructional Data Teams (IDTs). Schools that are successful at improving instruction and developing "accountable cultures" have principals who lead through the use of data (Portin, et al., 2009; Filbin, 2008; Fullan, 2008b).

BUILDING-LEVEL DATA TEAMS

While many or even most buildings now have some form of a building leadership team, the purposes of these teams are as varied as the buildings themselves. We will discuss the purpose of the Building Data Team (BDT) more in this section, but it is important to make a distinction between this team and other building-level teams.

The sole purpose of the Building Data Team (BDT) is to focus on the ongoing performance of students and the quality of instruction. By constantly examining the performance of all students in the building (by grade, subject, and course), the Building Data Team (BDT) assesses the overall effectiveness of the Instructional Data Teams (IDTs) and the specific shared strategies that everyone is learning to use well, the strategies agreed to in the Instructional Data Teams (IDTs), and any other interventions being used by the building. Rather than waiting for quarterly or annual summative data, the Building Data Team (BDT) reviews formative data and makes recommendations for actions in a more timely fashion.

Membership of the Building-Level Data Team

The membership of the Building Data Team (BDT) is critical. It should be large enough to represent the multiple perspectives within the school but not so large that it slows down the learning processes of the team. Usually the numbers vary between 8 and 10 members.

Initial selection of the team should be made by the principal and include:

- The principal.
- Representation from each grade level in elementary schools and from each department at the secondary level (depending on the size of the school, this may include selected representation).
- Other staff members who serve in leadership positions; e.g., instructional coaches, special education teachers, ELL teachers, and other support staff.
- Teacher union representation.
- Opinion leaders.
- If possible, an outside facilitator from the district office or external to the district.

The inclusion of an outside facilitator is at the discretion of the principal; however, this is highly recommended, especially when the team is new and just starting. We and other researchers have found that "most schools cannot improve instruction and achievement without some outside help, whether from the district office or some other external partner" (MacIver and Farley-Ripple, 2008, p. 66).

The principal should chair the Building Data Team (BDT); however, there can be a cochair who rotates over time. Being the "chair" does not equate to being the designated "leader." Most staff members will already defer to the principal too much. While it may be appropriate at times to use positional authority to help people follow their own structures, schedules, procedures, norms, and protocols, the goal of the team is to develop more leaders within the building.

Purposes and Functions of the Building Data Team

Just as with the District Data Team (DDT), the primary purpose of the Building Data Team (BDT) is "the improvement of instructional practice and performance, regardless of role" (Elmore, 2004 , p. 66). To accomplish this, the Building Data Team (BDT) will need to assess and monitor:

- The ongoing progress of all students.
- The quality of instruction in the building.
- The effectiveness of the teacher/Instructional Data Teams (IDTs).

To achieve these outcomes, the Building Data Team (BDT):

- Based on the building data, develops a school improvement plan that focuses on a limited number of strategies aligned with the district's goals and strategies.

- Determines the needs and specific shared instructional strategies to be learned.

- Actively monitors the implementation and effectiveness of the shared instructional strategies (adult indicators) and their impact on student learning.

- Actively monitors the teacher-based teams (Instructional Data Teams [IDTs]) and their follow-through.

- Provides for and participates in professional development and provides additional learning supports to staff.

- Makes adjustments based on the data.

The first task of the Building Data Team (BDT), however, is to address the same questions posed to the District Data Team (DDT).

Initial Questions the Building Data Team Needs to Answer

The following list of questions should act as a starting point for the Building Data Team (BDT). Don't rush through them. These questions should provide for the foundation of your continued work. While the list is not completely linear, it makes some sense to work through each item sequentially. The answers to the questions should form a roadmap for the Building Data Team's work.

1. What were your improvement goals and strategies this year? Identify them.

2. How well did you do? How do you know?

3. How clear are you and the team on the school's need for improvement?

    - How much consensus is there on the need for improvement? Is there a sense of urgency with the staff?

    - Have you made any measureable gains? How do you know?

    - Do you need to? For which subgroups?

    - Do you know which teachers *are* being successful now? Do you know why?

- Do you know which teachers are *not* being successful right now? Do you know why?

- Do you know which students are being successful right now? Do you know why?

4. How clear is each team member regarding the district goals and strategies for improvement and the aligned goals and strategies for the building?

  - How confident are you and other staff members regarding the strategies?

  - How many strategies are there?

  - How well are the strategies being implemented? How do you know?

  - How do you assess if the strategies are being effective (when they are being implemented)? Which data do you collect? How do you collect these? How often? What is done with these results? What actions have you taken? What student work do you look at?

5. What, how, and when do you provide professional development or other supports? Feedback?

  - How do you measure the effectiveness of your professional development? How do you assess if staff members are implementing the strategies? How do you know if the strategies are working?

  - How do you know if people need more?

  - What do you provide if people need more?

  - What other supports do you provide? Have they been successful? How do you know?

6. Does the Building Data Team (BDT) have a systematic way of learning in the school?

  - How do you identify and replicate success?

  - How do you reduce or shorten failure?

  - What supports for differentiated professionals are provided (observations, modeling, coaching, etc.)?

7. Do you have Instructional Data Teams (IDTs) by grade, department, and course?

  - How well are they functioning? How do you know?

- Are students making improvements as a result?
- Do you monitor their effectiveness? How? How often?
- What supports does the Building Data Team (BDT) provide (structures—time, protocols, etc.; training and facilitation)

Primary Strategies to Successfully Address the Questions

Chapter 2 provides a more comprehensive review of the improvement framework; however, in this chapter we focus on how the framework is applied to the building. It is important to understand that the framework is primarily implemented at the building level, and, as such, we will reiterate some important recommendations.

Use Data to Identify the Critical Needs of Schools and to Assess Ongoing Progress

Over time, the Building Data Team (BDT) will use a variety of data sources to assess the overall progress of the school. However, team members should begin this process by looking at whatever current assessment data they have available. At a minimum, this should include state assessment results, benchmark or quarterly data that are available from the district, and any formative assessment data that are available (e.g., common formative assessments, DIBELS data).

The outcome of the initial data review is to gain clarity, focus, and ownership for the improvement initiatives for the school. The Building Data Team (BDT) needs to clearly align the school improvement work behind the district goals and strategies. There should be a tightly coupled alignment between the district goals and strategies and the building goals and strategies. A caveat, however, is that if the district has not limited and focused its goals and strategies, then the Building Data Team (BDT) members need to do this work themselves. As we outlined in Chapter 2, having too many goals and strategies results in fragmented efforts and limited improvement.

Data on Instructional Strategies: Top–Down Strategies

Once the building moves to implementation of its strategies, there are two other data sources that the Building Data Team (BDT) needs to review in an ongoing way: implementation data and effectiveness data.

Implementation Data

As mentioned in Chapter 1, one of the biggest challenges that most schools and districts face is the lack of deep implementation. In our work with hundreds of districts, the ability to implement deeply and effectively has proved elusive for most districts and buildings. Whether this is due to a lack of accountability, or just a lack of planning, most districts and buildings do not collect, analyze, or act on their own follow-through of their improvement strategies. Consequently, they rely on their own or others' impressions, beliefs, or intuitions, and as a result, leaders never accurately assess how effective they are with their own implementation. This is a critical gap in data collection.

The Building Data Team (BDT) should collect data frequently on how well the improvement strategies are being implemented. Depending upon the strategies chosen, this could include a variety of data sources, such as walk-throughs, lesson plan reviews, student work samples, etc. This will usually require the development of some form of data collection tool such as rubrics, observation checklists, and so on. At a minimum, however, the principal, along with members of the Building Data Team (BDT), should decide what data need to be collected, how to collect these data, and how often to collect and report the data back to the staff on the depth and quality of implementation. Reporting back to the staff on a frequent basis should become a regular form of feedback regarding your progress.

Effectiveness Data

While it may be appropriate for the Building Data Team (BDT) to use state assessment results to make initial decisions about building goals and strategies, the Building Data Team (BDT) will need ongoing data to determine the effectiveness of its strategies and the progress of students and the school. Many districts use quarterly benchmark assessments as a part of this ongoing data review; however, over time it will become more important that the Building Data Team (BDT) guide the progress of the Instructional Data Teams (IDTs) in the use of common formative assessments. Because we know that "there (is a) greater emphasis in higher performing schools on ensuring that staff systematically monitored student progress" (Robinson, 2007, p.14), this should be a high priority for most Building Data Teams (BDTs).

This book is not the place to go into detail on the use of common formative assessments except to say that there is clear consensus in the research on the power of using formative assessments, and especially common formative assessments. In fact, recent research reviews have identified common formative assessments as the single most powerful strategy in improving student achievement and teacher learning (see Shepard, et al., 2005; Ainsworth and Viegut, 2006; Marzano, 2007; Hattie, 2009).

Data on Instructional-Based Data Teams: Bottom–Up Strategies

The Building Data Team (BDT) also needs to collect, analyze, and act on data regarding the effectiveness of the Instructional Data Teams (IDTs). If the Instructional Data Teams (IDTs) are following the process outlined in the following chapters, then there should be minutes available from each team to review. There also should be some common assessment data that are available to review, as well as the specific instructional practices team members have agreed to implement in their classrooms. The principal and the other members of the Building Data Team (BDT) should monitor and collect data on the follow-through of these practices in the classroom. These data should be presented and reviewed by the Building Data Team (BDT).

In addition, because many of the members of the Building Data Team (BDT) will also be members of Instructional Data Teams (IDTs), they should have first-hand knowledge of how well the teams are functioning. These members should report at each Building Data Team (BDT) meeting on the specific work of each of their teams, including the common student needs being addressed, instructional practices they've committed to using, how they will assess student learning, and how effective the teams have been in following the process. They should also identify if the teams need interventions or supports.

Using data at the building level serves many purposes; one of the primary purposes, though, is to personalize learning for every student. Data alone will not cause teachers to change their practices. It is only when teachers personalize this data to their own students that they begin to "own" the data.

Focus Your Goals and Strategies

Put simply, most district and building improvement plans have too many goals and strategies to be implemented well. As a result, most people within districts and schools cannot even tell you what the goals and strategies are in their improvement plans. An easy and quick test of the viability of your current building improvement plan is to informally ask staff members, "Can you tell me what our improvement goals are? Can you identify the specific strategies we are trying to implement? How often do you focus on the strategies?" If the answers to the questions show that less than 90 percent of the staff members know what the goals and strategies are, there is a pretty low likelihood of your being successful in meeting your goals. If staff cannot even identify what the improvement goals and strategies are, the likelihood of making any progress toward the goals or strategies is minimal when people don't even know what those goals and strategies are! Unfortunately, all too often building-level improvement plans are not really developed for the building staff to use, but are developed for either the district or the state as a compliance exercise. In either case, most of the time they end up having a limited impact on the progress of the building.

As we discussed earlier in this chapter, there is a long, rich history of empirical research as well as a number of recent meta-analytic studies on the importance of goal setting for schools and school leaders (Robinson, 2007; Robinson, et al., 2008; Marzano, 2003; Marzano, Waters, and McNulty, 2005). When done well, establishing goals and expectations can have a significant positive effect on increasing student performance and learning.

Leaders in higher-performing schools develop improvement plans that are aligned with the district's goals and strategies, identify action steps aligned with the strategies, and set performance targets aligned with the goals and strategies. They also work to communicate the importance of the goals and strategies, and they hold staff responsible for following through on the expectations (Robinson, 2007; Robinson, et al., 2008; Marzano, Waters, and McNulty, 2005).

The purpose of the planning process is to identify a limited number of goals, strategies, and action steps that help everyone focus, and to have a process that allows everyone to learn from this focus. Reeves (2006) warns that "there is a new religion spreading like wildfire in school systems and state departments of education. The religion is 'Documentarianism,' and, with missionary zeal, its adherents believe that with just the right school improvement plan, or the right format, or with all the boxes completed in all the right places, the deity to whom they pray will grant educational miracles" (p. 61). He goes on to expound on the virtues of "ugly" plans. Reeves found that, when it comes to planning documents, "ugly beats pretty" (p. 63) every time in terms of student achievement. He concluded from his research that "the stunning finding is that the 'prettiness' of the plan—conformity to format requirements—is inversely (or should we say perversely?) related to student achievement" (p. 64).

The point to be made here is that gaining clarity on goals, strategies, and action steps can be a powerful tool. However, the planning process can also be misused, particularly if the outcome is the development of the plan itself, rather than the deep implementation of the strategies. The biggest mistake that leaders make in the planning process is that they try to develop plans to address every possible issue or funding source.

The purpose of using data is to help educators focus on identifying the most important priorities, and then to implement and evaluate the strategies to improve student achievement. Remember that having ten priorities is like having no priorities at all.

Implement Powerful, Shared Instructional Practices

Over time, most educators have come to accept the findings that not all instructional practices are created equal in terms of their impact on student learning. Therefore, not all teaching is equally as powerful, and, as a result, there are more effective and less effective schools. What many educators do not realize, however, is that there is a wide variance in the quality of teaching in both effective and less effective schools. Nye, Konstantopoulos, and Hedges (2004) found that there was greater variance in teacher effectiveness within schools than there was across schools. What this means for students is that their performance is more dependent on the teacher that they get than on the school that they attend. This results in what Hattie (2009) calls "life changing outcomes" for many students. "If a student is in one of the most effective classrooms, he or she will learn in six months what those in average classrooms will take a year to learn. And if a student is in one of the least effective classrooms in that school, the same amount of learning will take two years. Students in the most effective classrooms learn at four times the speed of those in the least effective classrooms" (Hanushek, 2004; cited in Wiliam, 2007, p. 185). This would be bad enough, but Hattie (2009) also found that "the effects of poor teacher quality tend to persist for years after a student has had such a teacher" (p. 117).

While differences in student background do matter, what is more important is what the teacher does. More effective teachers use more effective practices, and these practices make a significant difference in student learning. So the logical question should be, "How can schools and districts create learning opportunities so that all teachers can be highly effective?" Hattie (2009) says, "School leaders who focus on student achievement and instructional strategies are the most effective" (p. 83). Therefore, the principal and Building Data Team (BDT) leaders need to work actively to improve instruction.

In Chapter 2 we outlined two ways to identify high-quality instructional practices:

1. Develop your own list of effective practices.

2. Go to the research.

Develop Your Own List of Effective Practices

We would recommend that the Building Data Team (BDT) follow the same processes as outlined in Chapter 2; that is, identify and develop your own list of high-quality instructional practices and instructional frameworks from within your own building. While your list will be somewhat unique to your building, it may be helpful to provide some guidelines. We know, for example, that we get higher levels of student performance when teachers use "authentic pedagogy," or instruction focused on active learning, real-world contexts that require higher-level thinking skills, extended writing, and some forms of demonstration (Darling-Hammond and Bransford, 2005). As you develop your list, keep these findings in mind.

Marzano (2009) also cautioned that while starting with a narrow focus on individual strategies is appropriate, it needs to be done within the context of a common language of instruction that is comprehensive and robust. The point is, don't just randomly pick instructional strategies; choose strategies based on the needs of the staff and students in the building, and work with staff members to develop, understand, and use a broader instructional framework.

Go to the Research

In Chapter 2 we cite a number of researchers who talk about powerful teaching and learning in different ways (Marzano, Waters, and McNulty, 2005; Hattie, 2009; Darling-Hammond, et al., 2008; Wahlstrom and Louis, 2008). We recommend that the Building Data Team (BDT) review this information along with other research and then create opportunities for discussion and consensus on what highly effective teaching looks like. This discussion and consensus should then be extended to the whole staff.

Implement Deeply

In Chapter 2 we outlined in some detail the challenge of implementing the work deeply across the school and district. We also talked about the importance of implementing at a 90 percent level. This 90 percent standard is rarely met in schools or districts. One way to get deeper implementation is to focus on a limited number of strategies (one or two instructional practices, and the use of Instructional Data Teams [IDTs]). The second way to address this is by rethinking how we provide professional development.

For learning purposes, we want to focus on only two things—the implementation of the specific instructional practices we have chosen (top–down shared learning) and the implementation of the Instructional Data Teams (IDTs) (bottom–up collective learning). These two strategies are aimed at improving instruction by collectively learning more about instruction. It is critically important to remember that all of this work is meant to be part of a "learning agenda" for everyone.

The purpose of implementing the framework is to focus deeply on a few important goals and strategies and then analyze and learn how to foster learning across every classroom and school in the district. If we cannot implement a few things deeply and well, and learn from them, then the likelihood of our making progress is minimal. We therefore need to think about and present this work to all of our peers as "a learning agenda." As a reminder, we started this discussion with the recommendation that everyone would learn more about instruction.

Implementing the instructional strategies and Instructional Data Teams (IDTs) requires both formal professional development and ongoing training and support. As outlined earlier in this chapter, most professional development currently does not provide either the intensity or duration of support needed to impact either teacher practice or student learning (Darling-Hammond, et al., 2009; Hattie, 2009). Achieving changes in teacher practice and student outcomes requires more intensive, sustained learning and supports for teachers that focus on how well students are learning, and which students are learning (Darling-Hammond and Richardson, 2009).

Teachers only change their practices when they have the opportunity to develop a *collective* understanding of high-quality instruction and are provided with ongoing opportunities to *collectively* reflect, discuss, deliberately practice, receive coaching, and then adjust their teaching (Darling-Hammond and Richardson, 2009). While all of these factors need to be addressed when we think about effectively implementing the specific instructional practices and the Instructional Data Team (IDTs), the most critical factors are the opportunity to learn with other staff members and the opportunity for ongoing, "deliberate practice" and coaching. If we want to improve instruction in the classroom, we need to provide ample opportunities for teachers to learn collectively, practice the new skills, and get feedback on their performance.

Reeves (2010) cites a number of researchers who identify "deliberate practice" as the key to improved performance. Deliberate practice involves ongoing practice that focuses on learning specific tasks while receiving immediate feedback (including modeling, coaching, and self-assessment) to improve our performance.

Because the Building Data Team (BDT) has the responsibility to oversee the effective implementation of both the instructional strategies and the Instructional Data Teams (IDTs), the Building Data Team (BDT) needs to provide opportunities for ongoing, differentiated, professional learning and supports to all of the staff members within the building. If individual staff members or teams are not making progress, the Building Data Team (BDT) needs to work to identify the individuals and the problems they are experiencing and adequately address these learning needs. This is a very different role from that of traditional Building Data Teams (BDTs). The Building Data Team (BDT) needs to be able to accurately assess progress, strategize how to meet the learning needs of individuals and teams, and ensure the provision of differentiated supports in a way that moves the work forward. If the Building Data Team (BDT) is ineffective in having the school make progress, then the District Data Team (DDT) needs to intervene and work directly with the Building Data Team (BDT) to identify what other supports or strategies might be more effective. Remember—both teams share the responsibility and accountability for effective implementation and progress.

Monitor and Provide Feedback and Support

One of the biggest gaps in implementation for most schools and districts is the lack of ongoing monitoring and feedback. It is impossible to assess how well the instructional practices or the Instructional Data Teams (IDTs) are being implemented without some form of frequent monitoring. White (2009) found that "schools with explicit monitoring achieved at higher levels than schools where monitoring was assumed or implied" (p. 12). He found that schools and districts that made significant progress specifically addressed a number of monitoring issues, including:

- What would be monitored? (What data need to be collected on how well the strategies are being implemented, and what data will be collected to show if the strategy is making a difference in student performance?)
- How will the practices be monitored? (Observations, artifacts, reports, etc.)
- When and how often will the practices be monitored?
- Who will be responsible for monitoring and reporting the progress?

The Building Data Team (BDT) will need to develop implementation indicators and monitoring processes that identify what effective implementation looks like and address the questions in the list.

The most important thing for the Building Data Team (BDT) to remember about monitoring is that monitoring is a tool to provide feedback to the staff and to the Building Data Team (BDT) regarding their progress in implementation. Fullan (2008a) cautions us that negative monitoring does not work! If monitoring is seen as a way to catch and persecute people, it will only increase resistance. The purpose of monitoring is to help staff see where they are in the implementation cycle and to give the Building Data Team (BDT) guidance on the right next steps and on what supports may be needed.

Learn, Inquire, and Replicate Success

All of this work is about learning. Instructional-based Data Teams are meant to provide teachers with the opportunity to collectively reflect, adjust, and improve their teaching. The Building Data Team (BDT) serves a similar purpose except that its focus is on improving instruction throughout the entire building. The goal of both is to develop a continuous-improvement process that is grounded in inquiry, reflection, and action. Most schools do not have a well-established process for inquiring and learning from their improvement efforts except for the final analysis of whether what they chose "worked" or "did not work." Traditionally, schools have not examined either the causes (i.e., what did the adults do or not do well?) or the effectiveness of the professional developments and supports provided. Without this happening, it is difficult for schools to learn or make progress.

In Chapter 2 we discussed the concept of learning organizations and referenced Reeves (2006), who found that schools that were higher in inquiry performed three times higher than schools that had lower levels of inquiry. Having the ability as a Building Data Team (BDT) to answer the questions of "what is working, and why?" and "what is not working, and why?" is profoundly important to the building's ability to make sustainable progress. If the Building Data Teams (BDTs) can learn from implementing focused instructional strategies and collaborative Instructional Data Teams (IDTs), then the Building Data Team (BDT) can refine and improve its implementation as the team moves forward.

CHAPTER 5

Instructional Data Teams (IDTs)

The primary purpose of the Instructional Data Teams (IDTs) should be "the improvement of instructional practice and performance, regardless of role" (Elmore, 2004, p. 66).

Darling-Hammond (2010) has explored the concept of teacher instructional data teams, which The Leadership and Learning Center refers to as IDTs, in depth and has concluded that "multiple studies have found it useful for groups of teachers to analyze and discuss student performance data and samples of student coursework in order to identify students' most common errors and misunderstandings, reach common understanding of what it means for students to master a given concept or skill, and find out which instructional strategies are or are not working, and for whom" (p. 228). She goes on to say that "many studies have identified the collaboration associated with professional communities of teachers as a key element of successful schools.... With teachers operating in grade level teams that meet regularly, the school creates structures for examining student progress, as well as for creating a more coherent curriculum and allowing teachers to learn from one another" (p. 261). She also reported that "a number of large-scale studies have identified specific ways in which professional community building can deepen teachers' knowledge, build their skills, and improve instruction" (p. 229).

While there continues to be emerging research on the benefit of Instructional Data Teams (IDTs), positive outcomes are only achieved when there is clarity on the purposes of the teams, training in the process, active facilitation, structures, and supports.

TEACHER COLLABORATION

Pappano (2007) identified some specific tasks that require teacher collaboration, including:

- Identifying what students need to know and be able to do by the end of the year.

- Writing common formative assessments and collectively reviewing the results.

- Reflecting and identifying which classroom practices produce the best results.

- Agreeing on, adopting, and using the most effective practices.

DuFour, et al. (2008) have worked extensively with PLCs and recommend that team members "work together to clarify exactly what each student must learn, monitor each student's learning on a timely basis, provide systematic interventions that ensure students receive additional time and support for learning when they struggle, and extend and enrich learning when students have already mastered the intended outcomes" (p. 18).

MEMBERSHIP OF INSTRUCTIONAL DATA TEAMS

Instructional Data Teams are small groups of teachers who collaborate to improve instruction and accelerate student learning. In the two previous chapters, you learned about the purpose and membership of District Data Teams (DDTs) and Building Data Teams (BDTs). The composition of an Instructional Data Team (IDT) is quite different. In the other two tiers of teams, equal representation of stakeholders is important; therefore, there are many different "faces" on the Data Teams. Instructional Data Teams are comprised of teachers who have been carefully, selectively, and purposefully placed around the table, functioning as a team.

These teacher-based teams focus on academic achievement and are driven by common academic standards. While we will talk more about the role of standards in the Data Teams process, it's important to know that common standards drive an instructional Data Team; therefore, members of the team must all teach the common academic standard, at the same time within the year.

There are also times when teachers can operate as a Data Team but teach different courses entirely. This is common for schools that have specialists, such as counselors, elective teachers, and others. The analysis of school-wide or district-wide data may pinpoint a "nonacademic" area in need of improvement, such as attendance, student engagement, or discipline. When teachers have a common focus, an art teacher, counselor, special educator, and physical education special-ist can sit around the table and have rich dialogue because they have a common purpose and focus.

Instructional Data Teams (IDTs) examine student work generated from a common formative assessment, which is measured with a common scoring guide or answer key. While this will be discussed more in later chapters, members of an Instructional Data Team (IDT) all use the same assessment, administer the assessment at the same time, and use a common scoring guide to measure levels of proficiency.

Teams are formed based on the criteria:

- All teachers on an Instructional Data Team (IDT) have a common standard or common area of focus.
- All teachers on an Instructional Data Team (IDT) administer a common formative assessment.
- All teachers on an Instructional Data Team (IDT) measure learning with a common scoring guide or answer key.

As teams are driven by the above criteria, membership may include:

- Grade-level teachers.
- Course or content-area teachers.
- Specialist or elective teachers.
- Counselors and support personnel.
- Data Team leaders.

Notice that the principal is not an ongoing, formal member of the Instructional Data Team (IDT) unless the team is not making progress. If the Instructional Data Team (IDT) is making progress (i.e., all students are making progress), then the dialogue that occurs in the meeting is an exchange of ideas and analysis of the teachers present at the meeting. Principals can certainly con-tribute to the dialogue, lending practical experience and expertise, but should only be a small voice in the Instructional Data Team (IDT) meeting, not the leader. Principals monitor the effectiveness by attending the meetings (not always in their entirety), providing feedback to the Instructional Data Team (IDT) leader and team, and observing and providing feedback as teachers use the agreed-upon common instructional strategies in the classroom.

PURPOSE OF THE
INSTRUCTIONAL DATA TEAMS

In previous chapters you read about the purposes of the District Data Team (DDT) and Building Data Team (BDT), which were quite comprehensive. The purpose of the Instructional Data Team (IDT) is quite simple: to improve teaching and learning and ensure that all learners and learning are accelerated on a continuous basis.

In order for Instructional Data Teams (IDTs) to achieve this purpose, they must use a systematic process. Instructional Data Teams marry two powerful practices (strategies addressed in previous chapters): using data well and teacher collaboration. Instructional Data Teams use a data-driven process—a Decision Making for Results process (Exhibit 5.1) that focuses on the collection and analysis of effect

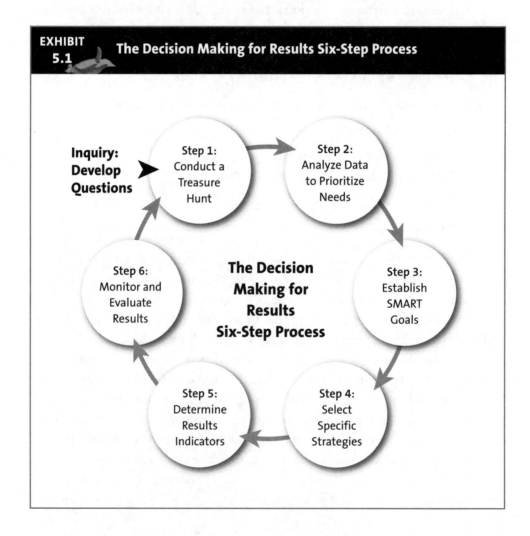

EXHIBIT 5.1 The Decision Making for Results Six-Step Process

Inquiry: Develop Questions

Step 1: Conduct a Treasure Hunt

Step 2: Analyze Data to Prioritize Needs

Step 3: Establish SMART Goals

Step 4: Select Specific Strategies

Step 5: Determine Results Indicators

Step 6: Monitor and Evaluate Results

The Decision Making for Results Six-Step Process

data (student performance data) and the impact of teacher action (antecedents leading to cause data). This systematic, structured process acts as the "fuel" for every Data Team. When Data Teams are implemented as a skeletal structure alone, the process will not work as effectively. Data Teams fuel the practice of collaboration by using the explicit data-driven process described below. School leaders need to actively monitor, support, and provide feedback. It is each team's effective use of the process that will lead to results.

The Decision Making for Results Process

Data Teams will become another failed initiative if there is not a systematic research-based process for making data-driven decisions. While Instructional Data Teams (IDTs) provide the structure for the powerful conversations and decisions around teaching and learning, it is the Decision Making for Results process (Exhibit 5.1) that powers every effective Data Team.

Inquiry

According to Reeves (2002), "Data-driven decision making begins by asking fundamental questions." Earl and Katz (2006) tell educators that data should drive their search for answers. While data may point us in the right direction, we should let our questions determine which data we examine. Therefore, our questions help determine what matters the most in the school-improvement process.

Instructional Data Teams (IDTs) are driven by questions that teams have about student learning. Building Data Teams (BDTs) inquire about learning and effective teaching, and District Data Teams (DDTs) use inquiry to gather information on teaching, learning, and leadership. Regardless of the subgroup of the Data Team focus, all teams are driven by inquiry.

Collecting and Charting Data (Treasure Hunt)

Data Teams use this first official step in the process to display disaggregated data and to look at learning by subgroups and levels of performance. According to Schmoker (1999), "You cannot fight what you cannot see." Data make the invisible visible. Not only do teams use data from a short-cycle common formative assessment; they also place a name with every number.

Leaders in the process can help to develop an environment of trust and respect knowing that the data will only be used to spark improvment in teaching and learning. Data in this process should not be used to rank, evaluate, or judge.

The data in this step should promote dialogue, lead teams to action, and inspire additional questions about student learning.

Analyze to Prioritize

Earl and Katz (2006) say, "Data by themselves are benign. Meaning is brought to data through the human act of interpretation. Data are symbols that stand for sets of experiences. Making meaning from data is about using the symbols to reconstruct the underlying experiences. Engaging with data in this way is an active process."

When Data Teams are given the time, the permission, and the authority to make meaning of their data, their level of analysis becomes much more thoughtful and the depth of their conversation reaches higher levels.

Teams examine performance trends and behaviors, which usually occurs in many collaborative meetings. However, the deep analysis that occurs in the IDT is what separates common conversations about numbers, or quantitative data, from collaborative dialogue that takes teams "beyond the numbers" (White, 2005). In other words, teams embrace the complexity of analysis and use their experience, knowledge, and expertise to form inferences which led to student learning. The hypotheses are data driven and reflect the root causes of performance, which are not based solely on the quantitative information.

At this point the IDT also engages in a process of determining the most urgent area of need for students, one that must be addressed in this data cycle.

Setting, Reviewing, and Revising Incremental Goals

Schmoker reminds us that "without explicit learning goals, we are simply not set up and organized for improvement or results" (1999). Goal setting is not a new practice for educators; in fact, most of us could recite the SMART goal chant. Typically, teachers view goals with two lenses: (1) as a summative measure of student learning, and (2) as a means to evaluate teachers.

IDTs take goal setting to new heights as they use incremental goals to analyze, monitor, and adjust professional practice—which is what makes this part of the process incremental. IDTs embrace the continuous-improvement cycle as they set, review, and revise goals throughout each data cycle (usually every two to three weeks). The obvious outcome for each goal is for all students to reach or exceed proficiency levels. However, because IDTs use an incremental process, acceleration is the expectation, and not all students are expected to reach proficiency levels in a short-term Data Teams cycle—this would depend on the proficiency levels that were disggreagated in Step 1.

It is through goal setting that IDTs develop the target and the structure in which they can work toward results. Incremental goals allow IDTs to monitor and adjust their practices. And it is also through incremental goals that teachers and students can celebrate their short-term gains.

Strategies

IDTs have structured and explicit conversation about instruction. By definition, this is the part of the process where there is a shift in the process from being student centered (Steps 1–3) to teacher centered (Steps 4–5). The Leadership and Learning Center defines the term "instructional strategies" as actions used by the teachers to impact the cognition of students. IDTs, first and foremost, focus on the root causes of student success and of student obstacles (Step 2). It is this lens that drives the dialogue regarding the strategies that are most likely to impact the root causes or misconceptions of student learning. Keep in mind, teachers also identify strategies that will extend and enhance those students who are acheiveing at proficient levels. It is also through this dialogue that teams filter research-based, action-oriented strategies that are targeted to the particular student need. Teachers share their secrets about teaching, they teach one another strategies, they share wisdom and experiences, and they may share research. While each teacher may contribute individual ideas, it is through collaboration that they commit to using the specific strategies that will best impact student learning.

Results Indicators

IDTs monitor the effectiveness of their strategies and the impact the strategies have on student learning. They do this by crafting Results Indicators. Results Indicators are statements that "paint the picture" (White, 2005) of effectiveness before students are assessed. Results Indicators illustrate effective teaching and the learning that follows. Teams can see the results of their actions through monitoring and know if the strategy is effective, or if the strategy must be tweaked and used in a different manner, or if the strategy is ineffective and therefore should not be used any longer. Results Indicators allow teams to make midcourse corrections and celebrate short-terms wins.

Monitoring

We've learned about the importance of monitoring in Section One, and in the Data Teams process this is the most often misunderstood, misused, and neglected step of the process. This step is often forgotten as it is not a part of the five-step meeting. It occurs during the alternate meeting. Teams monitor the agreed-upon strategies for effectiveness and impact on student learning. Teachers bring formal and informal evidence of student learning, and at this time they celebrate short-term wins and make midcourse corrections by tweaking their use of a strategy. At this time teams may also shift course entirely and commit to using a different strategy—one that may have a stronger impact on student learning.

Using the Process

This continuous process is used during every meeting, and it generally takes a team 45 to 90 minutes to use all five steps and leave with a plan of action. IDTs use the process as a continuous cycle every two to three weeks.

This data-driven, systematic, continuous process leads to gains in all areas: teaching, learning, and leadership. As stated earlier, this is a process that places the focus on students and student achievement as well as on teachers and instructional strategies. "The essence of data-driven decision making is not about perfection and finding the decision that is popular, it's about finding the decision that is most likely to improve student achievement, produce the best result for the most students, and promote the long-term goals of equity and excellence" (Reeves, 2002). Exhibit 5.2 provides a more detailed look at the Decision Making for Results process and the specific actions to be taken by Data Teams.

THE PRINCIPAL AS THE
INSTRUCTIONAL DATA TEAM ADVOCATE

An advocate believes, supports, promotes, and encourages. In our daily lives, we advocate for our children, our families, social causes, and even for our favorite sports teams. Principals, as the instructional leaders of the school, must be the lead advocates for IDTs, because IDTs are a powerful form of professional development and the key to improving teaching, learning, and leadership. Lee Crews, a principal in Ft. Bend Independent School District, recently said, "Success builds success. Schools become better places when they're working on the right work."

The right work is when teachers are given the time, opportunity, structures, and expectations to collaborate—when this occurs, great things happen. Therefore, principals must advocate for, implement, and sustain their efforts to focus on the Data Teams process.

Principals should foster and promote that vivid and rich image of staff members talking frequently about teaching and learning, sharing effective practices, and planning the materials and resources to support student learning and

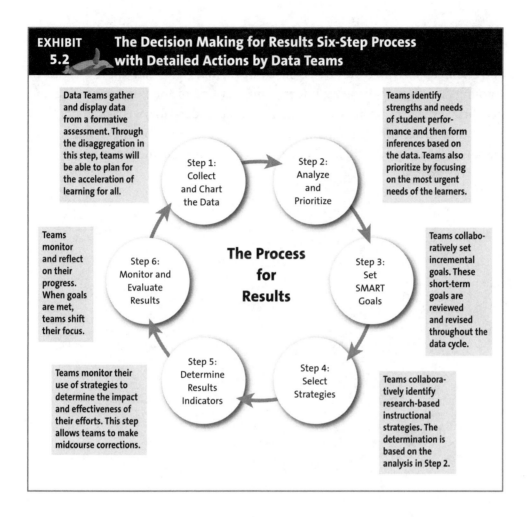

EXHIBIT 5.2 The Decision Making for Results Six-Step Process with Detailed Actions by Data Teams

The Process for Results

Step 1: Collect and Chart the Data

Data Teams gather and display data from a formative assessment. Through the disaggregation in this step, teams will be able to plan for the acceleration of learning for all.

Step 2: Analyze and Prioritize

Teams identify strengths and needs of student performance and then form inferences based on the data. Teams also prioritize by focusing on the most urgent needs of the learners.

Step 3: Set SMART Goals

Teams collaboratively set incremental goals. These short-term goals are reviewed and revised throughout the data cycle.

Step 4: Select Strategies

Teams collaboratively identify research-based instructional strategies. The determination is based on the analysis in Step 2.

Step 5: Determine Results Indicators

Teams monitor their use of strategies to determine the impact and effectiveness of their efforts. This step allows teams to make midcourse corrections.

Step 6: Monitor and Evaluate Results

Teams monitor and reflect on their progress. When goals are met, teams shift their focus.

instruction. They need to support the replication of that attitude of collaboration and collegiality with every teacher and thus reach every student. IDTs provide the structure for powerful conversations.

When implementing IDTs at your school, you should make informed choices and decisions about using a collaborative process to improve teaching and learning. Eliminate distractions or initiatives that do not support the improvement of teaching and learning in your building and focus on using IDTs as a professional development strategy that will positively impact student achievement.

"Principals cannot transform a school through their individual efforts. Creating a professional learning community is a collective effort, but that effort has little chance of success without effective leadership from the principal" (DuFour, Dufour, and Eaker, 2008).

Your leadership as a building principal will drive the success or failure of the IDT process. Capture your success stories, share your journey using your results, and celebrate the deliberate and positive impact that Data Teams have on student learning. This is a challenging undertaking but one of the most rewarding and beneficial experiences you will have as a building leader. How well you model collaboration, determine the right course, align the contributing systems, and empower the invested people will determine how effective the IDT structure will be in your school.

SECTION THREE

Making It Happen

Leading and Sustaining the Data Teams Process

Chapter 6 provides an overview of the necessary foundation of a Data Team: standards, assessment, and instruction. Oftentimes you'll hear educators associate the word "curriculum" with these terms; however, this chapter houses these practices in a construct embedded in the Data Teams process: standards, assessment, data analysis, planning, and instruction. You won't be able to find the specific components on a district or school "map," as the information is specific to each team using the process. This chapter is mostly geared toward the practice of Instructional Data Teams. It has implications for leaders of the DDT and the BDT, as one of their responsibilities is to monitor the work and results of Instructional Data Teams.

Chapter 7 introduces the structure and organization of the Data Teams process. Administrators will read this section to learn more about the roles and responsibilities of the Data Team leader and team members.

Read Chapter 8 to learn more about sustaining Data Teams through monitoring and celebration.

CHAPTER 6

Leading the Data Teams Process: Standards, Assessment, and Instruction

In the previous chapters of this book, we've discussed the framework for school improvement and the different types and functions of Data Teams. This section will focus on foundational components of Data Teams implementation and sustainability. The ideas presented here are applicable to leading this process at any level.

While it may be quite tempting to just "implement Data Teams," we caution against haphazard action, as there are considerations and practices that need to be in place for Data Teams to get results in improved teaching, learning, and leadership. The Teaching and Learning Cycle is a construct or visual structure used to house powerful practices of effective schools—a focus on Priority Standards, formative assessment, data analysis, and planning for instruction. While the construct is cyclical, there is a prescribed sequence for educators to ensure optimal teaching and learning (see Exhibit 6.1).

This visual structure outlines a comprehensive approach to teaching and learning:

- Standards drive our work, and Priority Standards give teams focus.

- Assessment measures our teaching and student learning.

   ◦ Common formative assessments measure student learning and the results of our instruction on a frequent basis.

- Analysis is needed to bring meaning to the data; teams use this step to go "beyond the numbers" and bring collective insight to data.

- In order to ensure that our instructional sequence is complete and correct, Data Teams use collaborative planning to deliberately and

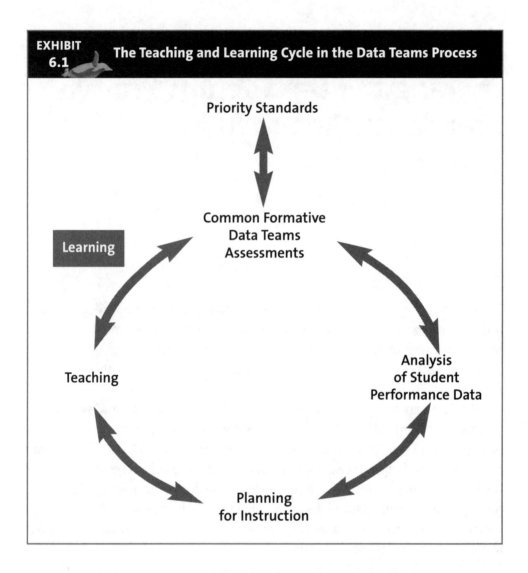

EXHIBIT 6.1   The Teaching and Learning Cycle in the Data Teams Process

explicitly determine strategies, resources, and processes that will best help the learners.

- Teaching is a science and an art. The science of teaching is practiced in the Data Teams process; the art is shaped when teachers return to their classrooms and work toward increasing student learning.

Standards provide fairness, equity, and excellence and should therefore drive our assessment and instruction (Reeves, 2002). Notice that the cycle begins with Priority Standards, because all teaching and learning should be driven by the learning expectations.

PRIORITY STANDARDS
IN THE DATA TEAMS PROCESS

When educators are faced with the challenge of trying to teach the vast number of academic standards within our systems, they are often overwhelmed. Popham refers to this mistake in *Unlearned Lessons* (2009):

> ... there is not enough time to teach what's represented by these excessive targets, and because students' mastery of those targets cannot be assessed in an instructionally sensible manner, the negative impact on U.S. classrooms is both pervasive and profound. Having too many curricular aims leads to off-target teaching and excessive test preparation and can, consequently, devastate a state's educational program.

As a leader, one of your greatest challenges is to help teams bring focus to their collaboration. While Priority Standards are targets for student learning, they are also guiding standards for Data Teams.

Teachers have known for a long time that there are too many standards to teach well. Marzano, Pollock, and Pickering (2001) found that the allotted time required to teach the required amount of standards would amount to more than 15,000 hours of instruction, which—in Marzano's words—would transform our system of a K–12 to one of K–22. That estimate still doesn't take into account the allotted "learning" time it takes for students to develop a depth of understanding of the concepts and the skills embedded in each standard. The study tells us that by trying to cover all of the standards, teachers are only able to superficially address the standards and not provide the depth of understanding and higher-level thinking skills that are necessary to apply this new knowledge.

Because it is not possible to teach all of the standards and benchmarks, districts and schools need to work with their staff members to prioritize the learning outcomes for their students. The process is often referred to as powering or prioritizing standards (Ainsworth, 2003a).

Power Standards, or Priority Standards (Ainsworth, 2003a), are those that provide endurance, leverage, and readiness for learning (Reeves, 2002). Reeves also defines Power Standards as those that provide students with a solid foundation for learning new content; Power Standards are assessed on a high-stakes test. Priority Standards are the safety net that ensures that *all* students are able to demonstrate proficiency in the standards that matter the most for student success. However, it is difficult to accomplish this feat, as any teacher will tell you, if we are trying to teach the breadth of the Power Standard during every instructional cycle. Priority Standards are a document of the concepts and skills that matter the most for students. However, the process of prioritizing is what is most powerful for educators, because teachers are collaboratively determining which standards are the most important for student success.

Data Teams also take the time to "make sense" of the Priority Standard— to bring clarity to what students must understand and demonstrate. To accomplish this, teams must take the time to "unwrap" (Ainsworth, 2003b) standards or break the performance statement into digestible chunks for effective and efficient student learning. This is a process that Data Teams use to create formative assessments.

Exhibit 6.2 serves as an illustration of how a team uses prioritization and the "unwrapped" standard to determine a "road map" for teaching the standard. The left column represents the state or national standard. The middle column reflects the prioritization of standards. The school or district determines the power of each strategy by deciding which skills and concepts have leverage, provide foundational understanding, and are enduring concepts. Lastly, the column on the right reflects an explicit picture of the "unwrapped" standard. The "unwrapped" chunks will guide the assessment design and will translate to specific learning outcomes.

As you can see in Exhibit 6.2, an "unwrapped standard" can serve as the foundation for a curriculum map of a Data Team. Teams may decide to narrow the focus even further in order to teach specific concepts or skills that are measured in short cycles of two or three weeks. The example in Exhibit 6.3 illustrates this process.

Exhibits 6.2 and 6.3 are examples of how teams prioritize the teaching and learning of the concepts and skills. This should not be a random act of prioritization. Rather, teams should consider the specific needs of the subgroup of students based on their analysis of data. They also need to consider concepts and skills that have leverage in other areas of study, such as literacy, problem solving, and cognitive skills, as well as concepts and skills that will be assessed on high-stakes tests.

This priority/"unwrapping" process allows each Data Team to create a framework that allows the Data Team to personalize its road map. Priority Standards provide opportunities for students to develop "deep learning" (Hattie, 2009), and "unwrapped" Priority Standards allow teachers and students to learn, process, shape, and celebrate small bits of learning.

Reeves (2002) reminds us that collaborative teams add value to standards by closely examining, analyzing, synthesizing, and *prioritizing them*. This process is

	Power Standards— Specific Substandards or Indicators (What Students Must Know and Be Able to Do) Example: Grades 5–8	"Unwrapped" Standards— Translated into Digestible Chunks of Learning (Data Team Focus Areas)
Standard/Strand		
• Students apply thinking skills to their reading, writing, speaking, listening, and viewing	• Recognize an author's or speaker's point of view and purpose, separating fact from opinion • **Use reading, writing, speaking, listening, and viewing skills to solve problems and answer questions** • **Make predictions, draw conclusions, and analyze what they are reading, hearing, and viewing** • Recognize, express, and defend a point of view orally in an articulate manner and in writing • Determine literary quality based on elements, such as author's use of vocabulary, character development, plot development, description of setting, and realism of dialogue *Note:* Power Standards are bolded	**Power Standard #1** Concepts: • Viewing skills • Problem-solving skills Skills: • Use • Solve • Answer Context: • Reading • Writing • Speaking • Listening **Power Standard #2** Concepts: • Making predictions • Drawing conclusions • Analysis Skills: • Make • Draw • Analyze Context: • Reading • Viewing • Listening

EXHIBIT 6.2   How Data Teams Use Prioritization and "Unwrapped" Standards to Determine a Road Map for Teaching the Standard

Colorado Department of Education

EXHIBIT 6.3   Narrowing the Focus for Data Teams

Standard that Reflects an Added Value	Data Team Priority List
Power Standard #2 Concepts: • Making predictions • Drawing conclusions • Analysis Skills: • Make • Draw • Analyze Context: • Reading • Viewing • Hearing	1. Making predictions 2. Analysis of text 3. Drawing conclusions *Note:* Teams change focus standards when desired proficiency levels have been reached.

built into every Data Teams cycle so that teams deliberately examine their standards before determining assessment and instructional practices.

Primary Strategies for Leading the Focus on Learning through Priority and "Unwrapped" Standards at Different Levels in the Data Teams Process

The following strategies can guide Data Teams at different levels:

1. **District level.** Create opportunities for teachers to develop an understanding of the powering and "unwrapping" process. These teams of teachers will also create documents of power and "unwrapped" standards to be used district-wide. Select representatives from all schools, grade levels, and/or departments to lead this important work. Use the "accordion model" (Ainsworth, 2003b) to prioritize and "unwrap" the standards. This model allows a small cadre of experts to do the first stage of work; it is then shared with colleagues around the district and input is elicited. When all feedback is received, the work of

the core group then begins to develop the final draft of "unwrapped" standards.

2. **School level.** Begin the process by involving the entire staff if possible. In elementary schools begin with one content strand; secondary-level schools can have multiple content areas. There are three objectives in this process: (1) to teach the purpose and process of prioritizing and "unwrapping" standards, (2) to establish procedures and processes when applying the Priority Standard and "unwrapping" process, and (3) to translate the work into the Data Teams process and infuse the Priority Standards into the Data Teams process. It's also very helpful to have vertical conversations in this process, because this leads to common understandings of expectations and proficiency levels. It also helps to eliminate any gaps, repletion, or omission of content learning standards.

3. **Instructional Data Teams.** If your district or school has not prioritized or "unwrapped" standards yet, use your high-stakes testing data to determine your urgent content area of need. Prioritize all of the major concepts within that standard. "Unwrap" these one at a time, before each Data Teams cycle.

ASSESSMENT

Teachers need to develop an understanding of assessment literacy. What are the different types of assessments? What are the different purposes of assessments? Teachers also need to reflect on the use of assessment in the classroom. Which assessments will provide teachers with the best information? Who is the primary audience for the assessment results? When and how do students receive feedback? It is important for teams to differentiate between the types of assessment used in our schools: formative and summative. While summative is used to measure end levels of learning, formative assessment is used to measure instruction and levels of learning during the instructional process.

Assessment and testing. Two very touchy and misunderstood concepts in education. While tests generally measure what students have learned and mastered, and are often used to assign grades ... assessments measure the impact of teaching.

HATTIE, 2009

Formative Assessment as a Process to Measure and Adjust Instruction

Formative assessment is a planned process in which assessment elicited evidence of students' status is used by teachers to adjust their ongoing instructional procedures or by students to adjust their current learning.

POPHAM, 2009

The evidence gathered during the assessment process must be used to adjust instructional strategies and approaches in the classrooms (Popham, 2009). Formative assessment is used to measure student learning *during* the instructional process. The information is then gathered to adjust and change our instructional strategies, approaches, and resources in order to have a stronger impact on student learning.

Teachers use formative assessment on a day-to-day and even minute-by-minute basis to gather information on the impact of their teaching. To put it simply, teachers continually evaluate whether their actions are positively impacting student learning. Effective teachers use a variety of informal methods to check for student understanding: questioning, student dialogue, and even nonverbal responses.

Teachers also use more formal methods of formative assessment such as quizzes, activities, and assignments. Another method used to measure student understanding is writing. Teachers use writing as a formative tool as it's a way to measure student learning. Teachers ask students to write so that they can reflect on their own knowledge, record their ideas, and grapple with the content (Peery, 2009). Performance tasks, structured dialogue, simulations, and projects are also examples of formative assessments used in the classroom.

Formative Assessment in the Data Teams Process

Data Teams should use assessment *for* learning (Stiggins, et al., 2004), with the purpose of collecting evidence along the way to a learning goal. Data Team assessments serve as a diagnostic tool for teachers, and allow teams to analyze student performance, set goals, and determine the most effective strategies for instructional intervention.

The assessment cycle in the Data Teams process includes pre- and post-instruction assessments that will provide information on the levels of learning that are occurring in the classroom. Data Teams should use assessments that are short-cycle measurements of student learning. These short-cycle assessments are derived from the concepts and skills identified in the "unwrapped" standard. The "unwrapped" standard is the driving force behind the creation of a Data Team assessment. These short-cycle assessments should take students no longer than 15 minutes to complete, because they are only meant to measure a subconcept or skill of the Priority Standard.

In the Data Teams process, most teams use Priority Standards. Since these standards require students to demonstrate a more complex understanding of the concept, assessment items would include a constructed response. The written response will also need to be measured with a rubric, or scoring guide. This will allow for specific feedback. On the other hand, when a Data Team is driven by a skills-based focus, a selected-response assessment is used to measure learning.

Exhibit 6.4 illustrates the ongoing cycle of assessments in the Data Teams process:

- Assessment #1—A pre-instruction assessment is administered before instruction begins. This measurement will provide evidence on students' levels of learning before instruction begins. It also serves as baseline data for the instructional cycle.

- Assessment #2—A post-instruction assessment is administered after teachers have used the agreed-upon instructional strategies. While the assessment is used to measure the level of learning that has occurred since the previous assessment, it is not used in a summative manner.

- Assessment #3—If goals were not met in the previous cycle, teachers continue the assessment process by administering another assessment that will provide information on student understanding of concepts and skills.

- Assessment #4—A formative assessment is administered to measure student learning.

  Note: Assessments for teams that have a focus on process-based skills (writing, reading, math, and science processes) act as a continuous cycle. The concept and skills are not changed in this instance, only the context or resources.

Exhibit 6.5 is an example of a Data Team Assessment Cycle.

It is recommended that schools create an assessment map to house a comprehensive picture of assessments at their school. This assessment map (Exhibit 6.6) illustrates the need to have a balance of both summative and formative assessments.

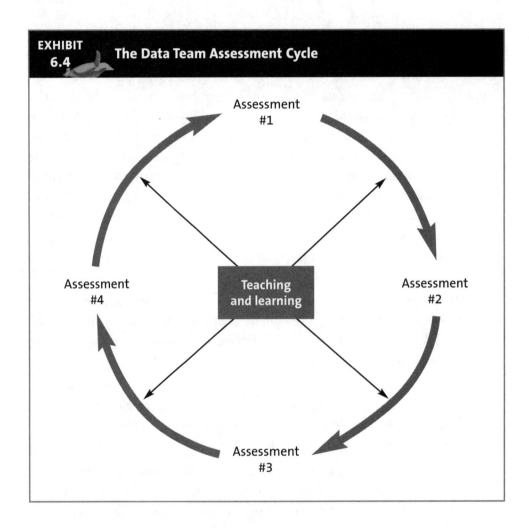

EXHIBIT
6.4   The Data Team Assessment Cycle

Teachers need to measure the knowledge and understandings that students have developed at the end of a course or unit and usually do so with summative assessment. These assessments measure a larger body of information; therefore, it takes additional time and opportunities for students to master the concepts and skills.

At the same time, teachers need to gather information about the learning that is occurring during (not after) the instructional process. These are the formative Data Team assessments—assessments *for* learning. The formative assessments measure the "unwrapped" concepts and skills from the Priority Standard, whereas the Priority Standard is usually measured with a summative assessment. Schools can use the formative assessments that Data Teams administer as "dipsticks," or predictors, of student success on a high-stakes summative assessment.

EXHIBIT 6.5	Example of a Data Team Assessment Cycle			
Focus Area	**Assessment #1**	**Assessment #2**	**Assessment #3**	**Assessment #4**
Literacy: Reading comprehension (pre-reading strategies) and expository writing (organization)	Reading*: Reading prompt—make predictions about the text in a written response *(Measured with a prediction and written-response rubric)*	Reading: New prompt about predicting text, new reading selection—respond in a written response *(Measured with a prediction and written-response rubric)*	Reading: New prompt about predicting text, new reading selection—respond in a written response *(Measured with a prediction and written-response rubric)*	Reading: New prompt about predicting text, new reading selection—respond in a written response *(Measured with a prediction and written-response rubric)*
Mathematics: Problem solving	Algebra: Algorithm and problem-solving prompt Geometry: Algorithm and problem-solving prompt *(Measured with an answer key and problem-solving rubric)*	Algebra: *New* algorithm and problem-solving prompt Geometry: *New* algorithm and problem-solving prompt *(Measured with an answer key and problem-solving rubric)*	Algebra: *New* algorithm and problem-solving prompt Geometry: *New* algorithm and problem-solving prompt *(Measured with an answer key and problem-solving rubric)*	Algebra: *New* algorithm and problem-solving prompt Geometry: *New* algorithm and problem-solving prompt *(Measured with an answer key and problem-solving rubric)*

*Text is adjusted to the reading level (strategies are being measured, not the reading level).

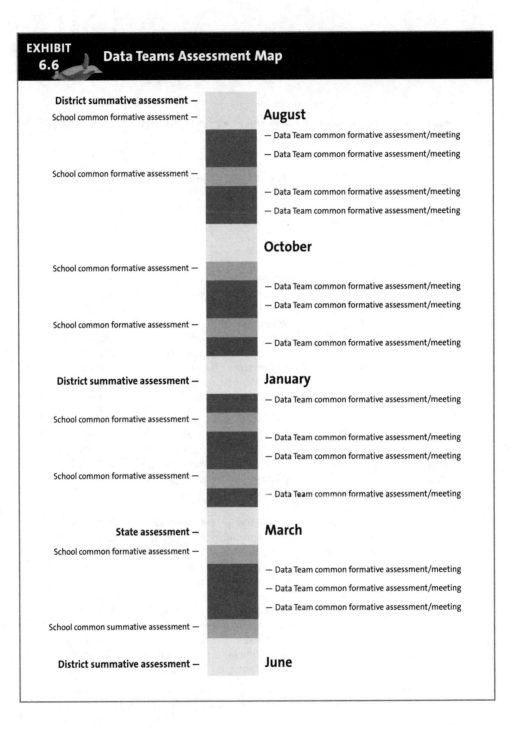

EXHIBIT 6.6   Data Teams Assessment Map

District summative assessment —
School common formative assessment —
August
— Data Team common formative assessment/meeting
— Data Team common formative assessment/meeting

School common formative assessment —
— Data Team common formative assessment/meeting
— Data Team common formative assessment/meeting

October

School common formative assessment —
— Data Team common formative assessment/meeting
— Data Team common formative assessment/meeting

School common formative assessment —
— Data Team common formative assessment/meeting

District summative assessment —
January
— Data Team common formative assessment/meeting

School common formative assessment —
— Data Team common formative assessment/meeting
— Data Team common formative assessment/meeting

School common formative assessment —
— Data Team common formative assessment/meeting

State assessment —
March
School common formative assessment —
— Data Team common formative assessment/meeting
— Data Team common formative assessment/meeting
— Data Team common formative assessment/meeting

School common summative assessment —

District summative assessment —
June

Primary Strategies when Leading the Focus on Assessment in the Data Teams Process

Use the following strategies to lead the focus on assessment in the Data Teams process:

1. Find the assessment leaders in the school. Have these teachers guide other teachers through "mini" staff development sessions that explore assessment as a topic.

2. Provide feedback to teachers on their use of formative assessments: as a process to gather information on the impact of instructional strategies and as a process to provide feedback to students. Collect data regarding for what and how teachers are using the information gathered.

3. Guide teachers in the creation of an assessment map. The assessment map should have both summative and formative assessments listed. (See Exhibit 6.6.)

Data Team members will become stronger consumers of assessments as they develop, identify, locate, and use these assessments to measure student learning. It is through experience, trial and error, and success that teams will increase the validity and reliability of their measurement tools.

As leaders guiding this process, it is important for us to make the connections between the summative and formative assessments administered at our schools. Summative assessments in a school will continue to serve as benchmarks of student success. Scores also serve as learning (or effect) data—evidence that our leadership collects toward meeting goals on a school improvement plan. Just as a Data Team collects formative assessment data on student learning, the formative assessment data that you use to monitor your school improvement plan should be the formative data collected by each IDT.

> *The evidence from holistic accountability systems is clear: classroom assessment, created and scored by classroom teachers, is the gold standard in educational accountability.*
>
> REEVES, 2004

Collaborative Scoring in the Data Teams Process

After administering the assessments described earlier, the Data Teams must then evaluate student performance based on common criteria. This is done prior to attending the scheduled five-step Data Teams meeting.

In the 2004 study by Reeves of 90/90/90 schools, he found that a "striking" characteristic of these successful schools was frequent external scoring of assessments. He also found that these schools were most successful when assessments were created and scored by a classroom teacher. He called this the gold standard in education.

It is recommended that Data Teams score the common formative assessment collaboratively. This practice helps teachers develop a common understanding of proficiency levels and, in turn, provides greater consistency when scoring student work and providing feedback to students. This practice of inter-rater reliability may be difficult for teams at first, but with practice they will become more consistent and will more quickly arrive at a common analysis of student work.

In the early stages of the Data Teams process, teams will have determined a small area of learning ("unwrapped" standards) that will drive their first Data Teams cycle. At the same time, teams will have developed a scoring guide, or rubric, that will be used to measure student learning. After administering the common assessment, teachers will come together (prior to the Data Team meeting) and score student work. This practice will help to bring reliability to the Data Teams process.

Involving Students in the Data Teams Process

Feedback is one of the most powerful influences on student achievement (E.S.=0.73) (Hattie, 2009). Feedback allows learners to respond to the following questions:

- Where am I going? This is the "unwrapped" standard (concepts, skills).
- Where am I now? This is evidence gathered from the formative assessment.
- How can I close the gap? This will include multiple learning experiences and feedback.

In order for feedback to be effective, it must be related to the learning target or task and reflect student performance toward that learning objective. That feedback must also be accurate, timely, and fair. Feedback can take many forms and happens during interchanges between student and teacher and student and student; it also occurs during self-reflection. Hattie (2009) cautions us against the second context, because 80 percent of feedback students receive is incorrect. His findings show that the most powerful feedback comes in the form of students self-evaluating their own progress toward achieving the learning goals.

Informal feedback can take the form of questions, nonverbal cues, and conversation—tools that classroom teachers use on a daily basis. In the Data Teams process, teachers continue to use these strategies as a way to measure instruction and provide students with immediate information on learning. Because Data Teams have a very specific focus, student feedback is targeted to the specific concept or skill from the "unwrapped" standard. The feedback is driven by the criteria on the scoring guide or by results of the item analysis.

Formal feedback may take place via conferences (small group and individual), written reflection, and self/peer/teacher evaluation of a task. Data Teams use all three methods within the process, and it is important that teams make feedback an explicit part of the Data Teams process. It should be used during the Data Teams cycle and after the post-instruction assessment is administered.

Strategies for Involving Students in the Data Teams Process

1. Help teachers to make the learning target (standard) very clear. As addressed earlier, students are involved in the process and are very aware of the Priority Standard and each "unwrapped" substandard that they will be learning.

2. Help students monitor their performance by creating and monioring personal goals.

3. Help teachers understand the practice of using feedback that provides students information on progress toward the learning target. Within each Data Teams cycle, there are multiple learning opportunities for students to shape their learning. Teachers are providing informal feedback on all of these learning experiences. Data Team assessments—the short-cycle or mini-assessments—are used as well to formally provide feedback on student progress toward the learning target.

Data Analysis in the Data Teams Process

Within the Teaching and Learning Cycle construct is data analysis. Teams are driven by the Priority Standards. They "unwrap" the standard to create short-cycle formative assessments, administer the assessment, and then collaboratively score the student work. The next step involves deep analysis of student performance.

Data is the heart of, or the basic foundation for, all of the work. The Data Teams process is structured so that data drive the actions of every team. In

Chapter 5 we described the Decision Making for Results process that teams use in the Data Teams process. The first three steps in the process use the collection of student learning data, or effect data. Because the final two steps of the process are focused on instruction in the classrooms, evidence is gathered on the effectiveness of instruction, the level of implementation, and the impact of instruction on student learning.

PLANNING FOR INSTRUCTION IN THE DATA TEAMS PROCESS

Collaborative Planning in the Data Team Cycle

Collaborative planning in the Data Team cycle is explicit and driven by data. It is the outcome of the meeting—of the five-step process. Data Team planning is driven by formative assessment data, deep analysis of student performance and short-cycle goals, along with deliberate and explicit selection of instructional strategies. Data Teams also plan to monitor instruction and the entire process.

We've learned that collaborative teams are much more successful than individuals. The Data Teams process breaks down barriers of isolation, and together teams solve problems and plan for ways to accelerate learning for all students.

Instructional Strategies in the Data Teams Process

The act of teaching requires deliberate interventions to ensure that there is cognitive change in the student.

HATTIE, 2009

The final phase of the collaborative approach to improving learning, as noted in the teaching and learning cycle, is the planning of instructional strategies, approaches, and resources (Step 4) to meet student needs identified through data analysis (Step 2).

The Leadership and Learning Center defines "instructional strategies" as "deliberate actions of adults that impact the cognition of students." Basically, it's what teachers do—the strategies they use—that impact student learning in a positive manner (Marzano, 2003; Marzano, Pickering, and Pollock 2001; Hattie, 2009; Zemmelman, et al., 1998).

First and foremost, Data Teams need to connect Step 4 (selecting instructional strategies) to Step 2 (analysis of student performance and prioritizing cognitive needs of students). Next, Data Teams need to be grounded in research-based strategies. Teachers must also have a deep understanding of the strategies and of the data that support the effectiveness and impact of the strategies on student learning. Then, teams must explicitly determine which strategies will have the greatest impact on student need.

As mentioned in Chapter 5, the rich conversation that occurs in the IDT meeting is powerful and it is a valuable professional development opportunity for teachers to talk about teaching and learning. The conversation is research based, the talk is structured, and in the end, teachers walk away with a targeted action plan that is accompanied by deliberate and explicit strategies. This professional learning opportunity allows teachers to "own" their professional development, share expertise and experience, and further develop their instructional practice. Teams appreciate learning from each other and collaborating for the benefit of their students. Good practice is replicated, and rich discussions about instruction become part of the learning culture.

When teachers leave the meeting, they have a common plan of action. However, the plan is meant to be implemented and revised based on the evidence of student learning. As Hattie (2009) points out, it's not good enough to just use a research-based strategy. Teachers need to be aware of whether it's working or not and be able to respond to the needs of students. Teachers self-monitor and evaluate and share results with teammates—this is actually an "alternate" meeting in which teachers use the evidence to determine if their target instruction has been effective. Teachers are "informing" themselves (Hattie, 2010). If their use of instructional strategies is not working, they make a midcourse instructional correction.

The Classroom Teacher in the Data Teams Process

The process described in the Teaching and Learning Cycle shifts at this point from the focus of a collaborative approach to one of the individual teacher. The Data Teams process promotes the "science of teaching," which is determined in Step 4, as well as the "art of teaching" (Marzano, 2007). Teams commit to using common instructional strategies, all of which should be research based. However, the manner of delivery will lie with the personal style and approach of the teacher. We want teachers to use their genuine and authentic approach to teaching, but with researched-based strategies.

The Data Teams structure is self-monitoring. It is used by the team, the teachers, and the students. If schools are really using this process as a continuous improvement cycle, the feedback received will affirm powerful teaching and leadership practices, will identify when a midcourse correction is necessary, and will provide real-time feedback to students. It is when principals, teachers, and students embrace Data Teams through the lens of the Teaching and Learning Cycle that true learning occurs.

Primary Strategies to Support Instruction in the Data Teams Process

Use the following strategies to support your teachers in the Data Teams process:

1. **Take an inventory.** What strategies do your teachers have an awareness of? What strategies do they have deep understandings of, along with evidence of their impact? What are the high-leverage strategies that teachers know and use in the classroom? What research-based strategies are they completely unaware of?

2. **Build capacity.** Develop the instructional capacity of the Data Team leaders. Rely on these experts to disperse learning to their teams.

3. **Use action research, book studies, and cadres** as structures to develop awareness of strategies.

4. **Use coaching** to help teachers develop a deep understanding of the strategies and receive feedback on their use of the strategies. Cover classrooms so that teachers can observe colleagues (shouldn't take more than 15 minutes to observe strategy and debrief).

5. **Model the use of research-based strategies** during professional learning time and in your monthly leadership meetings.

6. **Increase the amount of feedback you give teachers** on their efforts toward increasing achievement (Hattie, 2010).

THE POWERFUL IMPACT OF INSTRUCTIONAL LEADERSHIP

In earlier chapters we discussed the role of the instructional leader. We learned that instruction—what happens in the classroom—has the most powerful impact on student learning. However, next in line would be school leadership (Fullan, 2008b). Instructional leadership is cultivated when school leaders create opportunities for teachers to focus on instruction and use data to improve student learning (Fullan, 2008b).

In the Data Teams process, teacher leaders are the instructional leaders of their Data Team, school principals must be the instructional leaders of the BDT, and superintendents and central office administrators must be the instructional leaders of the DDT.

The Teaching and Learning Cycle is not inclusive to only student learning; it is a structure that houses effective practices. As you follow through the cycle, what should become clear is that all educators need to know more about standards, the use of Priority Standards, and, most importantly, what the critical learning is for students. At the same time, educators need to become much more deeply grounded in the importance of assessments to monitor ongoing student progress and to access the effectiveness of their own teaching. Assessment literacy is a necessary skill in today's schools. The third part of the cycle is the analysis of data. While most educators will agree that we have plenty of data, there is a distinct possibility that the ability to use ongoing data is critical if all students and all teachers are to make progress. Everyone has more to learn about instruction, and particularly about which strategies are most successful for the students in our schools. Each part of the cycle offers an opportunity for ongoing learning for all educators. Therefore, the expectation is that we will learn our way through the process. The process will result in learning for all educators.

CHAPTER 7

Leading the Data Teams Process: Structure and Organization

Creating the conditions for teams to work together toward a common purpose and a common cause can be a challenging process. Leaders guiding the Data Teams process must create the atmosphere and conditions for teacher collaboration and good use of data.

Before you begin the journey with Data Teams, it's important to define what you value in professional learning, as well as take inventory of your current practice:

- What do your collaborative teams currently look like?
- How are they formed?
- What processes do they use?
- What data do they use?
- How do these teams focus on teaching and learning?
- What results are these teams getting?
- Who guides this process?
- On a scale of 1 to 10 (1 being low performing), how would you rank your teams on their effectiveness?

Implementation is not about changing all of your current practices in professional collaboration. Rather, it is about first identifying effective practices, noting the strategies that are not yielding the desired results, and "pulling the weeds" to eliminate practices in collaboration and data use that are not effective.

The Data Teams process is meant to take these discussions about effective practices to a deeper level. Therefore, in addition to the questions above, the teams would specifically address:

1. Which specific instructional practices are most effective and why?

2. Which specific instructional practices are less effective and why?

The Data Teams process is meant to help everyone address these questions and follow through with the most effective practices.

As you read this chapter, please consider the structure and organizational components that are leading to your success—the antecedents that are correlated with effective collaboration and data use. Don't eliminate a practice if it's currently working for you—you've heard the saying, "If it ain't broke, don't fix it." Instead, celebrate the effective practices and/or consider ways to improve them to get better results.

On the other hand, when you are revisiting your responses from the questions that were posed, if you have an ineffective practice, don't complain about it or blame the principals, teachers, or parents. Do something about it. We can't afford to let ineffective practices linger. Because we know that Data Teams are an effective model, refine your Data Teams to get the best results possible. If you are new to the Data Teams process, this information will help you as you plan to implement Data Teams at the district or school level.

CREATING THE CULTURE FOR DATA TEAMS

Schools and districts need to be set up for success. Earlier, we talked about the need for creating a culture that embraces data and collaboration. Creating a school culture for Data Teams to thrive is critical. In *Data Teams Success Stories* (2010), Kristin Anderson incorporates the following quotes to frame school culture:

> "A set of common understanding around which action is organized . . . finding expression in language whose nuances are peculiar to the group" (Becker and Geer, 1960).

> "A set of understandings or meanings shared by a group of people that are largely tacit among members and are clearly relevant and distinctive to the particular group, which are also passed on to new members" (Louis, 1980).

Many of our clients attest to the importance of building a culture that will allow the Data Teams model to grow, prosper, and lead to the improvement of teaching, learning, and leadership.

Dolores Garcia-Blocker, Ph.D., Principal of Cooperative Arts and Humanities Magnet High School in New Haven, Connecticut, states, "The Data Teams process is at the core of my belief system for improving student achievement, not only for struggling students, but for the students who are functioning at high levels as well" (Anderson, 2010). She continues by saying that the Data Teams process must be embedded in the school culture because it is a process for school improvement.

John Hill, Ph.D., Director of Curriculum and Instruction in Elkhart, Indiana, refers to collaboration as "just the way we do business" (Anderson, 2010). His district enhances the culture of teamwork by intentionally making collaborative decisions at all levels. Just as we advocate for teaching educators how to use a data-driven process to make good decisions, collaboration must also be taught. Data Teams are not an initiative that teams "do." Data Teams are a model and process for improving teaching, learning, and leadership.

So, which do you do first—work on the culture or work on the practices? Work on the practices, because the use of new, more effective practices will create different, more productive relationships and will result in a more effective collaborative culture.

THE DATA TEAM LEADER

Behind every successful Data Team is an effective Data Team leader. This person is pivotal in the sustainability of the Data Teams model. Considerable thought is required to determine the characteristics, roles, and responsibilities of this leadership role.

Characteristics of an Effective Data Team Leader

While there are many characteristics of a strong Data Team leader, don't become discouraged if your leaders don't possess every characteristic. Remember, this is a model for professional development and it takes time to work at the exemplary level in every area. Teams will need much support and guidance, not always from you as the leader of a school or district. The Data Team leader will do the hands-on, day-to-day work with the Data Team.

With this knowledge, you must carefully consider the people who will guide your teams. After much practice, we've identified attributes and responsibilities that characterize an effective Data Team leader (Exhibit 7.1). These characteristics apply to leadership at any of the three types of Data Teams. The following list provides a more detailed description of these qualities.

Skilled Facilitator. The Data Team leader needs to be skilled in guiding conversation through analysis to action. Garmston and Wellman (1999) calls facilitation the "primary agent for adult group development that supports student learning." The Data Team leader needs to challenge assumptions, separate debate and discussion from dialogue, and provide intervention if the group is headed in the wrong direction.

Data Literate. The Data Team leader must activate collaborative knowledge and use of data. The leader needs to guide teams in using the systematic Decision Making for Results process and help teams bring meaning to

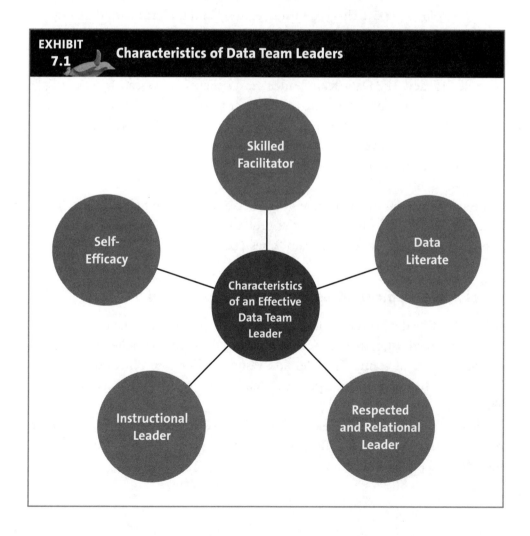

EXHIBIT 7.1   Characteristics of Data Team Leaders

results. This person doesn't need to be a "data nerd" but does need to understand and lead the productive use of data. This individual needs to be data literate in order to be a data leader.

Respected and Relational Leader. When Reeves talks about relational leaders (2006), he says that trust and credibility that stem from meaningful relationships are essential for leadership success. Keep in mind that we aren't saying that you need to have *Kumbayah* sessions or weekly happy hours; however, we are advocating that the Data Team leader have integrity, which is essential in gaining respect from colleagues.

Instructional Leader. Instructional leaders encourage and facilitate the study of teaching and learning. They facilitate collaboration, establish relationships, and use research to make decisions (Marzano, Waters, and McNulty, 2005). This is a misunderstood and underpracticed quality. Data Team leaders are the models of instructional leaders, because the position of the team leader requires you to be an instructional leader.

Self-Efficacy. The Data Team leader must believe that he can affect change. While self-efficacy may be related to self-esteem, leadership in the Data Teams process is not about feeling good about yourself. It's more about being confident in your skills and ability to effect change and to provide the leadership to get results.

As overwhelming as it may seem, it doesn't take a superman to lead a Data Team. It takes someone who believes in the process, believes in himself, and has the knowledge and skills to guide a team to results.

Roles and Responsibilities of the Data Team Leader

Exhibit 7.2 lists the primary roles and responsibilities of the Data Team leader.

The characteristics of an effective Data Team leader remain the same, regardless of the type of team. The roles and responsibilities are obviously different, because the function and purpose of each team are different. Leading a Data Team is not an easy task.

Just as Data Teams need leadership, guidance, support, and intervention, so does the Data Team leader. Be patient, provide support when necessary, and invest in this person and this role.

EXHIBIT 7.2   Roles and Responsibilities of the Data Team Leader

Data Team Leader	Roles and Primary Responsibilities	Caution
District Data Team Leader	• Ensures that all stakeholders' voices are heard • Facilitates the process for monitoring district improvement goals	• This person is not always the superintendent
Building Data Team Leader	• Facilitates the process of monitoring school improvement goals and IDT goals and results	• This person is not always the building principal (the principal may be the "chair" but not the Data Team leader)
Instructional Data Team Leader	• Facilitates the five-step meeting process • Provides immediate professional development within a meeting • Ensures that the team is using the process with fidelity	• This person is not an administrator • This person does not evaluate teacher performance

Strategies for Developing the Data Team Leader

Use the following strategies for success in developing a Data Team leader:

1. Choose one method for identifying Data Team leaders: recruit, assign, nominate, or recommend. Don't leave this to chance, because the effectiveness of the team will reflect the skill of the Data Team leader.

2. Create your job description of the Data Team leader. Include qualities for which you are looking, skills needed for the role, and the responsibilities of the Data Team leader.

3. Create a list of leaders in your school and district. Conduct a "force field" analysis of your staff and stakeholders. Note those who fit the descriptors of a Data Team leader. Pull the weeds from this person by distributing his other leadership responsibilities to others.

4. Provide learning opportunities for personal and professional growth. These leaders must be trained in the data-driven process as well as in the Data Teams structure in order to actively facilitate the Data Teams process.

5. Provide learning opportunities for the development of facilitation skills.

6. Conduct organizational meetings with your leaders to review the foundational, implementation, and sustainability components of the Data Teams process.

7. Create organizational notebooks for the Data Team leader that include background information on the processes, articles to support their learning, templates of the process, the school improvement plan, schedules, and assessment calendars. There should also be a place to house agendas, minutes, and results of each Data Team meeting.

ROLES AND RESPONSIBILITIES
OF DATA TEAM MEMBERS

Teamwork is most effective when members have a clear understanding of their roles and responsibilities. Members develop a shared accountability and leadership for the results of their processes. While teams in the Data Teams process have a designated facilitator, we recommend additional roles during the meeting. These roles should be determined during the initial stages of the Data Teams process and can be assumed on an annual basis or as rotating positions. Regardless, a schedule needs to be established so that precious meeting time is not spent on clarification of roles and responsibilities. Exhibit 7.3 describes various roles that need to be filled by Data Team members.

FORMING INSTRUCTIONAL DATA TEAMS

We talked about the formation of DDTs and BDTs in Chapters 3 and 4. This section is about forming IDTs. These teams should be created and organized in a

EXHIBIT 7.3	Data Team Roles	

Data Technician	Data Wall Curator	Recorder
• Gathers data from all team members • Creates tables/charts/graphs that represent assessment results to be used in the Data Teams meeting • Communicates results to appropriate stakeholders	• Posts incremental assessment data • Manages the creation of a narrative (cause information) that accompanies the numbers (effect)	• Takes minutes of the meeting using standard templates • Distributes minutes to team members and appropriate stakeholders
Timekeeper	**Focus Monitor**	**Engaged Participant**
• Makes sure team follows predetermined time frames • Keeps team members informed of available time per step	• Keeps dialogue focused on step in the process • Reminds team of purpose when necessary	• Responsibility of *all* team members • Contributes to dialogue • Commits to decisions of team • Respectfully poses questions • Uses active listening

manner to maximize teaching and learning. There are three key components behind the organization of an IDT:

1. A common core standard or focus

2. A common formative assessment

3. A common scoring guide or answer key

In Chapter 6 we explained the role that standards, assessment, and scoring of student work have in the Data Teams process. While each concept is important by itself, it is the combination of criteria that drives the organization of people and the formation of teams. Exhibits 7.4 and 7.5 are examples of how IDTs were formed based on the obvious structure of grade-level and department teams.

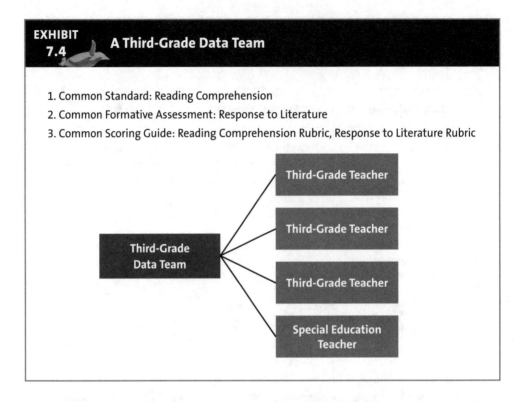

EXHIBIT 7.4   A Third-Grade Data Team

1. Common Standard: Reading Comprehension
2. Common Formative Assessment: Response to Literature
3. Common Scoring Guide: Reading Comprehension Rubric, Response to Literature Rubric

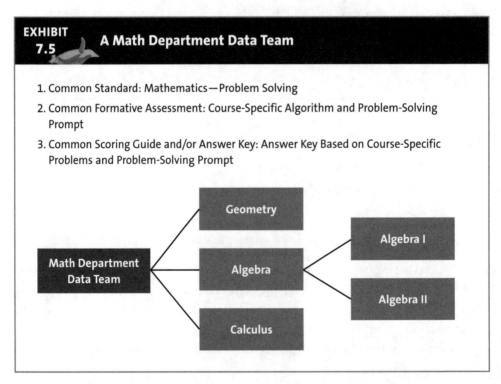

EXHIBIT 7.5   A Math Department Data Team

1. Common Standard: Mathematics—Problem Solving
2. Common Formative Assessment: Course-Specific Algorithm and Problem-Solving Prompt
3. Common Scoring Guide and/or Answer Key: Answer Key Based on Course-Specific Problems and Problem-Solving Prompt

Teams that are formed within a department may include teachers who teach different courses but have the same instructional standard, as shown in Exhibit 7.5. However, within a department you may have several Data Teams that may be comprised of educators who teach the same course. For example, within a science department there may be several different teams: a Biology Data Team, an Earth Science Data Team, and a Chemistry Data Team. Although all of these teachers are in the science department, they are on a Data Team that is course specific and driven by standards within that course.

The more difficult challenge of forming teams comes with all of the "extra" teachers—those who don't necessarily have colleagues who teach the same course. We certainly don't recommend that teachers "opt out" if they don't have a common department or grade level. Data Teams are not optional; Data Teams are the primary form of professional development and the vehicle that drives school improvement. Data Teams are about improving teaching and learning; therefore, all teachers need the opportunity to collaboratively improve teaching and impact learning.

Exhibit 7.6 is an example of how teachers in different roles can support a standard that is a lifelong skill, and it is applicable to all teachers and learners.

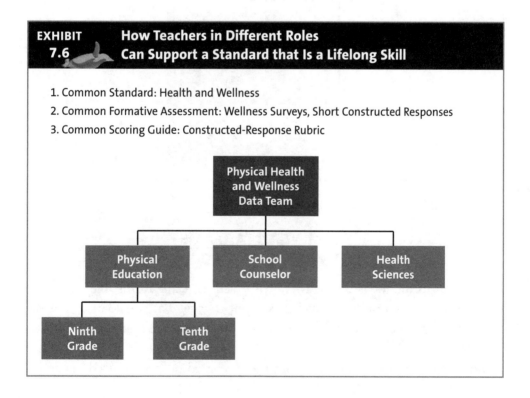

EXHIBIT 7.6   **How Teachers in Different Roles Can Support a Standard that Is a Lifelong Skill**

1. Common Standard: Health and Wellness
2. Common Formative Assessment: Wellness Surveys, Short Constructed Responses
3. Common Scoring Guide: Constructed-Response Rubric

Physical Health and Wellness Data Team

- Physical Education
  - Ninth Grade
  - Tenth Grade
- School Counselor
- Health Sciences

We've learned of the value of vertical articulation—collaborative time to talk with colleagues who teach the grades above and below the grades you teach. Vertical articulation allows educators to come to common understandings of standards, expectations, proficiency levels, and analysis of student performance data. Data Teams also use the vertical articulation model, but they use it more explicitly by using the five-step meeting process as a format in which to have those conversations. Vertical teams are formed using the same criteria.

Exhibit 7.7 is an example of a vertical team.

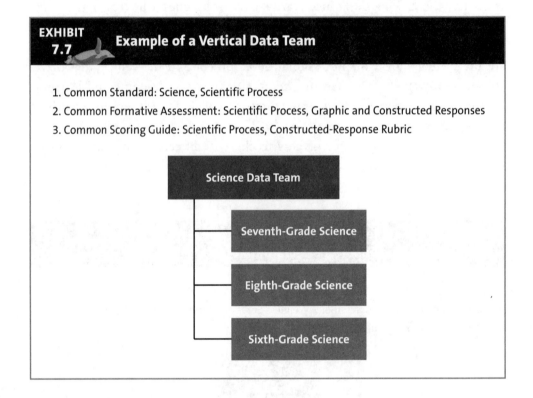

EXHIBIT 7.7   Example of a Vertical Data Team

1. Common Standard: Science, Scientific Process
2. Common Formative Assessment: Scientific Process, Graphic and Constructed Responses
3. Common Scoring Guide: Scientific Process, Constructed-Response Rubric

Science Data Team

Seventh-Grade Science

Eighth-Grade Science

Sixth-Grade Science

FORMING DATA TEAMS WITH A COMMON FOCUS

In addition to the focus on instructional practices, Data Teams may also have other areas of common focus, such as student engagement, attendance, motivation, and discipline. Other areas of focus that may be shared by all educators in the system include literacy and critical thinking standards. Data Teams with a common focus would follow a similar process based on specifc needs as determined by the examination of data. The criteria for organizing the team still apply. Exhibit 7.8 provides an example of a Data Team with a common focus.

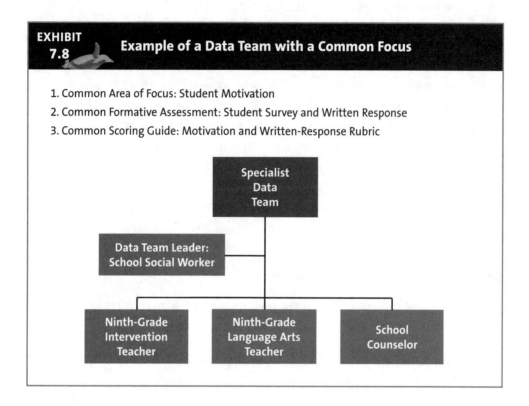

EXHIBIT 7.8　Example of a Data Team with a Common Focus

1. Common Area of Focus: Student Motivation
2. Common Formative Assessment: Student Survey and Written Response
3. Common Scoring Guide: Motivation and Written-Response Rubric

Specialist Data Team

Data Team Leader: School Social Worker

Ninth-Grade Intervention Teacher

Ninth-Grade Language Arts Teacher

School Counselor

Organizing your Data Teams for success is not always a pretty process; in fact, it's quite messy. You may use a variety of structures within your school, and your structure may change from year to year. Members of teams are organized by teachers who share common standards, assess those core standards using a common formative assessment, and evaluate student performance using common criteria.

FINDING THE TIME

The most important work in schools is student learning, followed by teacher learning. Time and focus are required in order to create opportunities for teacher learning. The Data Teams process is the most powerful form of professional learning because it directly links teaching practices with student outcomes. Therefore, it is critical that building leaders work to create ongoing time for their Data Teams.

Sadly enough, most of our schools are not designed for teacher learning. It is

imperative that teachers have adequate time to improve their instructional practices. High-impact learning requires deliberate practice (Reeves, 2010), and Data
Teams provide the structure for this deliberate practice.

Data Teams provide a link between teacher practices and student outcomes,
but they also provide an opportunity for teachers to practice specific teaching
strategies and to observe the impact of those strategies. *At the school and district
levels, deliberate practice is just as important for those serving in leadership roles.* We
tend to focus our energies on providing time and opportunity for teacher professional development but neglect our own personal and professional development.
Darling-Hammond (2010) refers to the structure used by Tony Alvarado when he
was leading schools in New York and California. The structure provided opportunities for principals to improve their practice through PLCs (comprised of
principals) and networking, attendance at conferences, mentoring, coaching, and
walk-throughs.

Scheduling in the Data Teams Process

When you are scheduling Data Team meetings, three tiers of meetings must be
planned: the DDT, the BDT, and the IDT.

Scheduling Time for District Data Teams to Meet

Let's revisit the purpose of the DDT as presented in Chapter 3:

> The primary purpose of the DDT is "the improvement of
> instructional practice and performance, regardless of role"
> (Elmore, 2004, p. 66). The DDT becomes the "guiding coalition"
> (Kotter, 1996; Fullan, 2009a) that leads the improvement work of
> the district forward. The DDT reviews the district's data, devel-
> ops the district improvement plan (including goals and strate-
> gies), ensures the provision of professional development and
> other supports, monitors the implementation and effectiveness
> of the strategies (or lack thereof) in each building, and learns
> how to replicate and sustain success. This team actively commu-
> nicates the improvement work of the district between class-
> rooms, buildings, and the district.

There are three primary functions of a DDT: to focus on quality instruction,
monitor the district improvement plan goals and strategies, and monitor the

implementation and effectiveness of school-wide strategies. Each of these requires data that must be collected, monitored, analyzed, and acted upon. The majority of DDTs meet on a monthly basis because they collect data on district improvement and school improvement on a monthly basis.

Scheduling Time for Building Data Teams to Meet

The sole purpose of the BDT is to focus on the ongoing performance of students and the quality of instruction. Once again, the purpose of the BDT should drive the frequency of meetings, not the schedule or availability of meeting time. We recommend that schools monitor school-wide improvement on a monthly basis; therefore, a BDT would need to meet monthly. These meetings usually take place in the week that follows an IDT.

Scheduling Time for Instructional Data Team Meetings

The purpose of the IDT is quite simple: to improve teaching and learning and ensure that all learners and learning are accelerated on a continual basis. How do we define "continual basis?" Is it once a year, four times a year, monthly, or weekly? Obviously, IDTs that meet frequently get better results than those that don't. Structured collaboration on the part of Data Teams must be scheduled. We recommend that IDTs meet no less than every three weeks; ideally, however, teams will use the five-step process every two weeks. Data Team meetings take 45 to 90 minutes and must be scheduled as one block of time. More and more school districts are redesigning their calendars to allow for large blocks of time for structured collaboration. However, if your school district calendar is written in stone, there are many options for scheduling time for Data Teams to meet. The length of Data Team meetings and actual dates of IDT meetings must be determined in advance.

Scheduling Time for Data Team Leader Meetings

These meetings are scheduled on a monthly basis and are attended by building administrators and Data Team leaders. This meeting has several purposes:

1. To monitor the progress of each Data Team.

2. To support Data Team leaders in their understanding of the process.

3. To provide professional development for Data Team leaders with book studies, reading of professional articles, sharing of strategies, and development of facilitation skills.

Strategies for Finding Time for Data Teams to Meet

The following ideas will help you find the time for your Data Teams to meet:

1. Use a late-start or early-out schedule.

2. Use teacher planning time.

3. Use traditional professional development time and break those into hours for team time.

4. Eliminate staff meetings; do business by e-mail; and use the time for meetings.

5. Use electives or specials classes for meetings.

EXHIBIT 7.9   **Comprehensive Data Team Meeting Calendar**

Time	Week 1	Week 2	Week 3	Week 4
August		BDT	DDT	DTL*
September	IDT	BDT	IDT DDT	DTL
October	IDT	BDT	IDT DDT	DTL
November	IDT	BDT	IDT DDT	DTL
December	IDT	BDT		
January	IDT	BDT	IDT DDT	DTL
February	IDT	BDT	IDT DDT	DTL
March	IDT	BDT	IDT DDT	DTL
April	IDT	BDT	DDT	DTL
May	IDT	BDT	IDT DDT	DTL
June	BDT	BDT	DDT	
July				DDT

*DTL refers to Data Team Leaders

6. Provide release time for teachers and have classes taught or covered by administrators, specialist teachers, or student teachers.

7. Pay teachers for team time after school.

Exhibit 7.9 shows a sample calendar for comprehensive Data Team meetings.

SET UP YOUR DATA TEAMS FOR SUCCESS

As a leader, your most important responsibility is student learning. To achieve this, you need to improve and strengthen instruction in the building. The research that we and others have conducted concludes that Data Teams are the most effective way to improve instruction and learning. Therefore, make Data Teams your highest priority.

If Data Teams are your "one thing," then put time and energy into creating the culture for Data Teams. Invest in your leaders and align all other practices to ensure that the model and practice of Data Teams are set up for success.

According to Fullan (2008b), " Leaving legacies is one area where individuals can make a direct contribution to improving themselves while simultaneously strengthening the system for the long run."

> *When teachers have structured opportunities to explore the nitty-gritty challenges of their practice through thoughtful exchanges with colleagues and in relation to relevant research, they rediscover the passion for learning and their own personal and professional growth that brought them into teaching in the first place.*
> HARGREAVES AND SHIRLEY, 2009

CHAPTER 8

Sustaining Data Teams by Monitoring the Process

The results are striking: when 90 percent or more of a faculty was actively engaged in the change initiative, student achievement results in reading, science, and math were dramatically higher than when the same initiative was introduced with only 10 percent of the faculty actively engaged.

REEVES, 2009

Reeves further concluded that the variable is not program based or tied to a consultant or a conference; the variable is implementation. The words "actively engaged" also should be highlighted. For it isn't until educators are actively engaged in the Data Teams process—in the process of improving teaching, learning, and leadership—that they will see results. And it isn't until group members are actively engaged that they will sustain the change.

We use the words "implement" and "sustain" quite a bit in education. To revisit Reeves—90 percent implementation doesn't happen with a district superintendent having nine out of 10 schools using Data Teams, or when a principal has nine out of 10 teams meeting regularly. The simple act of Data Teams implementation is quite easy. Anyone can change their team planning into "PLC" time or change the title of their PLC meeting to "Data Teams." It's quite simple to form a team, assign a leader, and give team members a meeting time.

On the other hand, when we define "sustain," the words "maintain," "continue," "carry on," "nourish," "support," "help," and "assist" come to mind. Implementation is a much easier and prettier task. It can be exciting, new, and even a breath of fresh air. It's sustaining the journey that may require blood, sweat, and even a few tears. Sustaining the Data Teams journey is a messy process, and there are many roadblocks to overcome. We have found that the practices needed to sustain the Data Teams process in good times and in bad are:

1. Monitoring

2. Feedback

3. A focus on results

4. Celebration

5. Using Data Teams as a professional development model

1. MONITORING IN THE DATA TEAMS PROCESS

Data Teams, and Data Team leaders, need continual feedback on their practices. While teams should be self-monitoring and seek feedback from colleagues, feedback from administrators who are supporting the process can provide information that will allow educators to refine their practices as a Data Team. In order for feedback to be effective, it must be timely, specific, and prescriptive, and it must respond to the following questions:

1. Where are we going? What is our purpose? What are the greatest needs of our students? What are our greatest needs as a team? The performance of an exemplary team is described in the rubric (Exhibit 8.1). Teams that exhibit the exemplary behaviors get high achievement results as a result of strong instruction and use of the Data Teams process. Effective teams continually do a "reality check" to ensure that their work is headed in the right direction and their work as a team is aligned with the mission of the school/district. This does not happen by chance, because teams that see great gains use collaboration and data to define specific needs and make decisions that will help all students.

2. Where am I now? Using the performance behaviors described in the rubric, what's the current state of the team? How effectively are team members using each step in the process? How is the use of data defining the current state of collective instructional practice? How are data used to define a baseline of learning for students?

3. How will we close the gap? Teams need to identify which behaviors are necessary in order to become a stronger team. Data Teams, at all levels, are action oriented. The strategies chosen by a team are research-based professional practices in leadership, instruction, organization, and processes. Effective teams are not comfortable with the status quo; rather, they are continually working to ensure that all teaching, learning, and leadership are accelerated. Teams continually monitor the use of strategies to ensure they are having the desired impact and to measure the results of their efforts.

The Data Team Rubric

Rubrics are designed so that learners can see what success clearly looks like. These tools are designed with specific success criteria that describe levels of performance. They are intended to provide measurable and specific feedback on progress toward a learning goal. Data Teams use rubrics to self-monitor performance and to offer specific feedback to peers. The Data Team rubric describes the performance criteria of each type of team: the IDT, the BDT, and the DDT. The criteria are specific to the purpose, function, and processes used by each team and should be used before, during, and after each meeting. The criteria describe proficient and exemplary use of a collaborative data-driven process.

Special thanks to Tony Flach, our colleague at The Leadership and Learning Center, for his creation of the instructional, building, and district rubrics. These valuable tools provide powerful feedback to all Data Teams.

Instructional Data Team Meeting Rubric
The Six-Step Instructional Meeting

The Decision Making for Results process was described in detail in Chapter 5. The most important feedback a leader can provide is on the use of the five-step meeting or the six-step Data Teams process described in Exhibit 8.1. This exhibit outlines the success criteria for an effective Data Teams meeting. Each step in the process is clearly described with criteria that are performance based and measurable. Teams should use the rubric to assess their progress and to provide feedback to the team in order for their practice to continuously improve.

The feedback gathered from measuring the IDT practice with the IDT rubric (Exhibit 8.1) can be used in a variety of ways and will be discussed later.

Monitoring Building Data Teams

In Chapter 4 we described the composition, purpose, and processes of the BDT. Just as the IDT monitors the effectiveness of its work, so does the BDT. Exhibit 8.2 is a rubric for an abbreviated set of performance criteria of an effective BDT. The Leadership and Learning Center has an extended rubric that further describes the practices of the BDT.

Monitoring District Data Teams

Because the primary purpose of a DDT is to improve teaching and learning, this team should also be monitoring the effectiveness of its practice. While the IDT primarily monitors its effectiveness within the five-step meeting, and the BDT

EXHIBIT 8.1	Data Team Rubric—Meeting Components	

Step	Proficient	Exemplary All Proficient Criteria PLUS the Following:
Step 1—Collect and Chart Data	• Data are assembled in discussion format prior to start of meeting	• Results are disaggregated according to specific subgroups present in the school
	• Results include number, percentage, and names of students at multiple performance levels (e.g., Goal, Proficient, Close to Proficient, Intervention)	• All team members, including support personnel who may not be able to attend meeting, have results
	• Data are disaggregated by grade-level standard if multiple standards are included on the assessment in order to support specific analysis	• Data are triangulated (multiple sources of data included that further illuminate students' knowledge and skill in the area being examined)
	• Data are disaggregated by teacher	
	• Data support timely, specific, and relevant feedback to teachers and students to improve performance	
	• Data include student work samples from the assessment being reviewed	
Step 2—Analyze Strengths and Performance Errors or Misconceptions	• The inferring of strengths and needs is based on a direct analysis of student work	• Prioritized needs reflect areas that will have impact within multiple skill areas
	• Analysis includes comparison of student work samples to targeted "unwrapped" standards	• Needs inferred for intervention group are categorized according to a hierarchy of prerequisite skills
	• Strengths and needs identified are within the direct influence of teachers	
	• Team goes beyond labeling the need or the "what" to infer the "why" or root cause	
	• Strengths and needs are identified for each "performance group" (i.e., strengths and needs for "Close to Proficient Students," for "Far to Go but Likely Students," etc.)	
	• Needs are prioritized to reflect those areas that will have largest impact within subject areas (if three or more needs are identified; otherwise, prioritization may be implied)	

EXHIBIT 8.1   **Data Team Rubric—Meeting Components** *(continued)*

Step	Proficient	Exemplary All Proficient Criteria PLUS the Following:
Step 3—Goals	• Establish, review, or revise a goal	• Targeted needs have impact in multiple skill areas; e.g., "identifying supporting details"
	• **S**pecific targeted subject area, grade level, and student	• Intervention students have a goal related to prerequisite skills necessary for proficiency
	• **M**easurable area of need is established, and assessment to be used is identified	
	• **A**chievable gains in student learning based on the consideration of current performance of all students	
	• **R**elevant goal addresses needs of students and supports school improvement plan	
	• **T**ime frame is established for learning to occur and the subsequent administration of the assessment	
Step 4—Instructional Strategies	• Strategies directly target the prioritized needs identified during the analysis	• Strategies selected impact multiple skill areas
	• Strategies chosen will modify teachers' instructional practice	• Strategies include modeling of how selected strategies would be implemented
	• Strategies describe actions of the adults that change the thinking of students	• Team anticipates/discusses acceptable, ongoing adaptations to strategy implementation ("if … then …"); *strong connection here to Results Indicators*
	• Team describes strategies for each performance group	• Team evaluates its capacity to use the selected instructional strategy and identifies needed resources, and so on.
	• Team agrees on prioritized research-based strategies that will have greatest impact	
	• Descriptions of strategies are specific enough to allow for replication (i.e., implementation, frequency, duration, resources)	

EXHIBIT 8.1	Data Team Rubric—Meeting Components *(continued)*

Step	Proficient	Exemplary All Proficient Criteria PLUS the Following:
Step 5—Results Indicators	• Results Indicators are created for each selected strategy	• Establishes interim time frame to monitor the implementation of the strategy
	• Describes what the teacher will be doing if the strategy is being implemented	• Clear and detailed descriptions that allow others to replicate the described practices
	• Describes what the students will be doing if the strategy is being implemented	• Specific enough to allow teachers to predict student performance on next assessment
	• Describes the anticipated change in student performance if the strategy is having the desired impact on the prioritized need	
Step 6—Monitoring Meeting	• a. Teachers bring student work samples that provide evidence of strategy implementation	• a. Multiple work samples are included that show the progression of strategy implementation over time
	• b. Teachers describe their implementation of the strategy, including frequency, direct instruction/modeling, and feedback provided to students	• b. Teachers observe colleagues in their use of the strategy and discuss observations during this meeting
	• c. Teachers examine the student work samples to determine the quality of strategy implementation	• c. Teachers discuss other situations in which the strategy may be used
	• d. Teachers examine the work samples to determine whether the strategy is having the desired impact (effectiveness)	
	• e. Teachers support each other in the use of the strategy through specific dialogue, modeling, planning, and so on.	
	• f. Teachers discuss the effectiveness of the strategy, including whether to continue, modify, or stop the use of the selected strategies	

Keep in mind that this same rubric can also be used by central office teams using the IDT process.

EXHIBIT 8.2   Building-Level Data Team Meeting Rubric

		4: Exemplary	3: Proficient	2: Progressing	1: Not Meeting Standards
Structure		• Team is comprised of all stakeholders: principal, representatives from all instructional teams, teacher leaders, building union representatives, parents	• Team is comprised of some stakeholders who do not have instructional positions	• Team is comprised of only IDT leaders	• Team is comprised of building administrators
		• Team meets bimonthly for 60–90 minutes	• Team meets monthly	• Team meets quarterly	• Team meetings are not scheduled and occur sporadically
		• Roles of members are clearly defined and shared	• Roles and responsibilities are clearly defined	• Building administrator assigns the roles of team members	• Roles and responsibilities are not identified
		• Agendas and minutes reflect the discussion of the meeting	• Agendas and minutes reflect the topics of the meeting	• Agendas are used, but the minutes don't always reflect the meeting discussion	• Agendas and minutes are not used
Meeting		• Cause (team instructional strategies) data are examined at each meeting	• Cause data (monthly) of teachers are examined at each meeting	• Cause data are not consistently examined	• Cause data are not examined
		• Effect (formative student learning results) data are examined at each meeting	• Effect data (monthly) are examined and represent both summative and formative results	• Summative effect data (quarterly) are examined	• Effect data are not examined
		• Data are disaggregated by IDTs, student subgroups, and teacher	• Data are disaggregated by IDTs	• Data are disaggregated by grade level or department	• Data are not disaggregated
		• Progress toward school improvement goals is monitored and evaluated	• Progress toward school improvement is monitored and evaluated monthly	• Progress toward school improvement is monitored and evaluated quarterly	• Progress toward school improvement goals is evaluated annually
		• Midcourse corrections are made as a result of the examination of data and reflect practices in leadership, organization, and professional development	• Midcourse corrections are made on a monthly basis and reflect practices in leadership, organization, and professional development	• Midcourse corrections are made on a quarterly basis and reflect practices in leadership and organization	• Midcourse corrections are made annually and reflect practices in organization

EXHIBIT 8.2   **Building-Level Data Team Meeting Rubric** (continued)

	4: Exemplary	3: Proficient	2: Progressing	1: Not Meeting Standards
Meeting	• Clear evidence that instructional practices are modified based on data • Clear evidence that classroom and student data are used to identify the most effective teaching practices • Effective teaching practices are collected, discussed, documented, and shared • Clear evidence that teachers and leaders are replicating best practices continuously • Clear evidence that changes in teaching and leadership strategies are associated with improved results	• Evidence that instructional practices are modified based on data • Evidence that classroom and student data are used to identify the most effective teaching practices • Effective teaching practices are collected, discussed, and documented • Evidence that teachers and leaders are replicating best practices • Evidence that changes in teaching and leadership strategies are associated with improved results	• Little evidence that instructional practices are modified based on data • Teaching practices are not always discussed • Little evidence that teachers and leaders are replicating best practices • Little evidence that changes in teaching and leadership strategies are associated with improved results	• No evidence that Instructional practices are modified using data • Teaching practices are not discussed • No evidence that teachers and leaders are replicating best practices • No evidence that changes in teaching and leadership practices are associated with results
Affect	• Environment is always free from fear • Mutual encouragement and exploration are present • All voices are heard and encouraged at each meeting	• Environment is free from fear • Mutual encouragement is present • All voices are heard at each meeting	• Environment is not always free from fear • Mutual encouragement is not always in practice • All voices are not always heard	• Environment is not free from fear • Mutual encouragement is nonexistent • All voices are not heard

EXHIBIT 8.3	District-Level Data Team Meeting Rubric			

	4: Exemplary	3: Proficient	2: Progressing	1: Not Meeting Standards
Structure	• Membership includes all those described in "proficient" plus community stakeholders on appropriate subcommittees • Team meets twice monthly for 90–120 minutes • Roles and responsibilities are so well internalized as to be interchangeable • Agendas and minutes reflect the topics of the meeting and are publicly displayed within 24 hours	• Membership includes superintendent, senior district leadership, bargaining unit representatives, building administrators, and teacher representatives • Team meets monthly for 90–120 minutes • Roles and responsibilities are clearly defined • Agendas and minutes reflect the topics of the meeting and are publicly displayed	• Membership includes some district representatives and partial representation from schools with limited decision-making authority • Team meets quarterly for 90–120 minutes • Roles and responsibilities are assigned and static • Agendas and minutes are used but are not consistent in representing actual discussion and/or are not readily available outside of the team	• Membership includes partial district and school stakeholders with little or no decision-making authority • Team meetings are not scheduled or held consistently • Roles and responsibilities are unknown or misunderstood • Agendas and minutes are rarely or never used
Meeting	• Effect data are analyzed and meet the requirements for "proficient"; they include information regarding the results of district strategies (i.e., changes in adult practice occur as a result of professional development) • Cause data related to key district strategies are analyzed and include quality indicators for every adult action • Strengths and needs focus predominantly on adults within the system and on the relationship of the adult needs to student performance	• Effect data are analyzed and include a mix of aggregate and disaggregate information needed to monitor overall district status and identify areas of successful practice or urgent need (outliers) • Cause data related to key district strategies are analyzed (i.e., functionality of IDTs) • Specific strengths and needs, particularly in adult actions, within the influence of system personnel are identified and prioritized	• Effect data are analyzed and include aggregate information to monitor overall district status and may include some individual disaggregation by school • Cause data related to key district strategies are sporadically available and analyzed • Strengths and needs identified are not consistently within the influence of system personnel and may include some discussion of adult practices	• Incomplete effect data are analyzed and include aggregate information to monitor overall district status • Cause data related to key district strategies are not available, nor is there an awareness of a need for these data • Strengths and needs identified are limited to student results and are not consistently within the influence of system personnel

EXHIBIT 8.3	District-Level Data Team Meeting Rubric (continued)			
	4: Exemplary	**3: Proficient**	**2: Progressing**	**1: Not Meeting Standards**
Meeting	• Analysis of data identifies underlying or root cause for prioritized needs and the impact of that cause on other areas of need	• Analysis of data identifies underlying or root cause for prioritized needs	• Analysis of data tends to stop with identification of areas of concern and does not address underlying causes	• Analysis of data tends to stop with identification of areas of concern and does not address underlying causes
	• Direct impact between school and district SMART goals is analyzed	• District SMART goals are monitored and adjusted as needed	• Status of district SMART goals is monitored	• Status of district SMART goals is monitored annually
	• Strategies are chosen to promote changes in professional practices that impact multiple areas	• Strategies are chosen to promote changes in professional practices connected to improving student performance	• Strategies are chosen for others to implement and may not relate to the actions of district-level personnel	• Strategies chosen place accountability on one group within the district
	• Results Indicators are precise enough to allow for "live" corrections in actions prior to next DDT meeting	• Results Indicators are created that describe adult actions related to implementation of selected leadership strategies and the anticipated changes in adult performance that provide evidence of successful implementation	• Results Indicators are created that describe improvement in state and district assessment results	• Results Indicators are not described
	• Environment is free from fear	• Environment is free from fear	• Environment is not always free from fear	• Environment is not free from fear
	• Mutual encouragement is present	• Mutual encouragement is present	• Mutual encouragement is not always in practice	• Mutual encouragement is nonexistent
	• All voices are heard at each meeting	• All voices are heard at each meeting	• All voices are not always heard	• All voices are not heard

monitors the meeting in addition to the structure and affect, the DDT monitors system-wide school improvement and the processes they use within the meeting (see Exhibit 8.3).

2. PROVIDING FEEDBACK IN THE DATA TEAMS PROCESS

Feedback provides teams with information on the effectiveness of their work. Teams need to receive feedback on the effectiveness of their collaboration and the way in which they are using data—both cause and effect—to improve teaching, learning, and leadership.

Rubrics are an effective tool when teams and leaders collect data and then act on the information. The formative data should be collected at each Data Team meeting through the reflection process. The frequent collection of data will allow teams to monitor and make midcourse corrections on their practices as a Data Team. Data should be collected in the form of individual self-reflection, team reflection, and/or from a colleague or administrator who is not a member of the team. Analytic criteria are used in the rubrics; therefore, teams can more clearly pinpoint areas of strength and need in collaboration, use of data, and impact of their work.

Reeves (2006) says that it's an absolute waste of time if you gather information on adult practices and student learning and then fail to act on it. While the Data Teams rubrics were designed to help schools and districts monitor their practices, they were also designed to help teams improve their practices. Feedback in the Data Teams process is most effective when:

1. It focuses on the performance of the team. The performance behaviors described in the rubrics are clearly measurable and therefore easily identified.

2. It is descriptive and detailed. Because teams are using rubrics with analytic performance criteria, descriptive data are gathered and then used. The descriptive nature of the rubric will allow for feedback that is very specific to team strengths and that will identify a precise area of need for the team.

3. It is easily understood. Teams will develop an understanding of the Data Teams process primarily by *using* the process. However, before teams begin, they need to have a clear understanding of what an effective Data Team looks like and how it functions.

4. It is timely. The timeliness of Data Teams feedback should coincide with the frequency of meetings. Therefore, if teams meet every week, they should be using the rubric, gathering feedback, and reflecting on their performance on a weekly basis.

Feedback is the most powerful when it is timely and used as a tool for self-reflection on the team's performance. However, if you are a leader who is observing a Data Team and providing feedback on its performance, there are a variety of ways in which you can use the data to provide feedback:

1. Provide immediate oral feedback during the meeting, but be careful not to disrupt the flow of the team. If your input is respected, then your contributions will seem more genuine and purposeful. If your feedback is more corrective, then it won't always impact the team in a powerful way.

2. Provide written feedback to the team and to individuals. Teams like receiving immediate feedback; however, personalize your feedback by selecting one or two areas from the rubric and provide feedback on their strengths and help the team to determine next steps for improvement.

3. Use coaching to provide feedback. Your feedback may be specific to one or two members of the team, in which case a private coaching session may be more appropriate. Use the data gathered from observations to guide the dialogue.

4. Use the Data Teams feedback service by The Leadership and Learning Center. Teams, schools, and districts may submit videos on their use of the meeting processes, and teams receive a report on the strengths and next steps in their use of the Data Teams process from a Center expert.

Regardless of the type of feedback a team receives, it needs to provide information so that team members can understand their strengths and their next steps. Teams become motivated and empowered when they can respond to the questions: Where are we going as a team? Where are we now? How will we close the gap? Effective feedback is a practice that will sustain the Data Teams process in your school or district.

3. RESULTS IN THE DATA TEAMS PROCESS

A focus on results is central to school improvement (Schmoker, 1999). Many think of results as an end product—one that leads to either celebration or disappointment. Obviously it is the formative focus on results that leads to improvement, acceleration, motivation, and change.

The use of Data Teams is a results-driven process that embraces incremental gains in teaching, learning, and leadership. Data Teams require a large investment in time, energy, and intellect by teachers, students, administrators, and all stakeholders. In short, they are hard work. Yet the results of Data Teams are phenomenal, as documented in *Data Teams Success Stories* (Anderson, 2010). Data Teams need venues to share the results of their hard work, because the results are what will sustain the momentum through motivation, feedback, and encouragement.

Data Walls and Data Halls

If you walk into a school or district of Data Team practitioners, you will most likely see a data wall. A data wall is a visual display of results of teaching, learning, and, indirectly, of leadership.

Data Teams are encouraged to display their results in student learning. Results are displayed in the form of a table, chart, or graph and reflect the gains in student achievement. To help stakeholders see the correlation between student achievement results and teacher actions, teams are encouraged to create a brief narrative that illustrates the adult actions that led to gains in student achievement.

Data walls should include the following:

1. Effect data—student achievement results. These displays should show growth over time while reflecting the Data Teams meeting cycle. If teams meet every two weeks, the formative student learning data would be displayed on the wall and reflect the achievement gains over those two weeks. Tables, charts, and graphs are often used as visual displays of the results.

2. Cause data—strategies of adults. While teams don't post the minutes of each meeting, it's important to include a narrative that describes the strategies used by each team to impact—or effect—student achievement. This seems to be more powerful when this is written by the team or even by students.

Data Boards

Data boards, or data displays, are often referred to as "the science fair for grownups," because the science fair board is typically used to display results. The primary purpose of using a display is to spark educational dialogue about teaching and learning.

Just as a data wall is used to house and share results, portable data displays are used for the exact same reason. When Reeves first designed this tool, the intention was for schools to house both processes and results:

1. External data: state, district

2. Internal data: school, classroom, grade level

3. Inferences and conclusions drawn from the data

The data board (Exhibit 8.4) should spark rich dialogue around learning, instruction, and leadership strategies and not just serve as a pretty display to impress stakeholders.

Data Fairs

Schools and districts host data fairs to celebrate student achievement gains as a result of teacher and leadership practices. A data fair is an event where educators bring their portable data boards to a venue, and it serves as an "exhibit hall." DDTs, BDTs, and IDTs will all bring data boards to the data fair.

Strategies for Using Data Walls, Halls, Displays, and Fairs

Strategies for using data walls, halls, displays, and fairs include the following:

1. Be very clear about the purpose of the data display. It should not be used as a punishment or for principal or teacher evaluation. The purpose of displaying data is to celebrate results and spark conversation. If your plan does not allow for this, then it's not considered a data display.

2. Display the right data. Display the data that represent your formative goals. Therefore, your data should represent growth over time, not only summative assessments.

3. Respect privacy. Teacher and student names should not be displayed— just team names.

EXHIBIT 8.4   **Example of a Data Board**

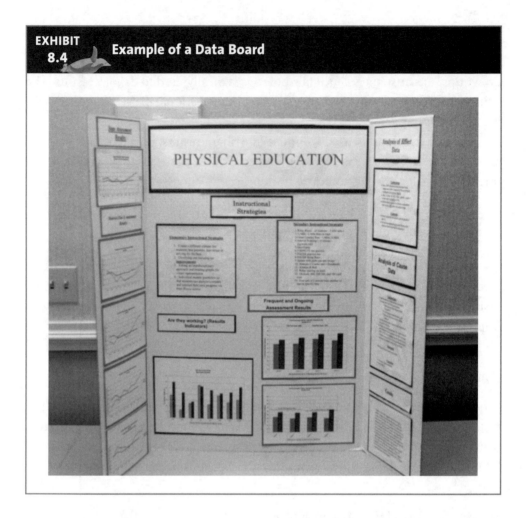

4. Use the displays to spark conversation. Don't let the display sit idly; it should become an interactive display and locale in your school or district. The display should be so compelling, not necessarily in the artistry but in the message, that all stakeholders want to stop, view, reflect, comment, and ask questions.

5. Let the portable displays speak for themselves. After you build a strong culture of data use and collaboration, the displays should serve as your faculty meeting, because the results will speak for themselves.

6. Make your data fairs special events. Include all stakeholders in the planning of the event. Make sure that it is representative of the teachers, students, parents, stakeholders, and leaders in the system. These events are often accompanied by food, music, and artistry that reflect the students in the system.

4. CELEBRATIONS

Schools and districts may celebrate annual events such as the release of state test scores, retirements, and national recognition of blue ribbon schools. However, the celebrations that are most valued by educators are those that give us short-term feedback and immediate wins: sports team victories, student spotlights, and monthly teacher recognition.

Data Teams are motivated by the celebration of short-term wins and recognition of efforts.

While the purposes of each Data Team vary slightly, *all* Data Teams have the purposes of improving instruction, leadership, and student learning.

In the first section of this book, we introduced a framework for school improvement and, through that, the importance of alignment of school improvement goals. When there is alignment throughout our system—short-cycle assessments, incremental goals, and measurable strategies—schools can celebrate both the implementation and the impact of their work. There's no need to wait until August for a district, school, or instructional team to celebrate results. The Data Teams model is structured so that progress and improvement are rewarded as results are achieved, not after results have been achieved.

Data Teams are hard work. Data Teams, whether they are at the school, district, or instructional levels, must embrace and celebrate results.

5. DATA TEAMS AS
A PROFESSIONAL DEVELOPMENT MODEL

The Data Teams process is an explicit, teacher-driven, ongoing, job-embedded, data-driven form of professional development that is highly effective. In *Reframing Teacher Leadership*, Reeves (2008) identifies the most influential force on teacher learning to be advice from colleagues. Data Teams are the model for teachers to offer one another advice. However, the "advice" isn't conversational or casual. The discussion or "advice" of the Data Team is driven by the deep analysis of student performance and then comprehensive dialogue about instructional and leadership action.

Professional development has a strong impact on teacher learning (d=0.62*) (Hattie, 2009). Hattie found that professional development does result in changes in teacher learning (d=0.90), but more often than not, this new learning has less

---

* "d" refers to effect size.

impact on teacher action (d=0.60) and even less impact on student learning (d=0.37). Teacher reaction toward professional development also has a minor impact (d=0.42).

He found that professional development must be job embedded, continuous, rigorous, and challenging. This means that leaders must support follow-up on the use of the practices and observe classroom practices of teachers in order to provide feedback.

Hattie (2009) also found that having teachers meet in a professional learning-type structure was not enough to impact student learning. To be effective in their follow-though, teachers need an explicit structure in which to house these conversations—Data Teams (Gallimore, et al., 2009; Saunders, et al., 2009).

In addition to Reeves and Hattie, Linda Darling-Hammond (2009) describes effective professional development as intensive, ongoing, and connected to instructional practice. She recommends that schools become places where all teachers are learning together. This, in turn, will result in increased learning for all students. In order to achieve this level of professional development, she recommends that schools have common times for teachers to meet. She also found that sustained and intensive professional development for teachers correlates with gains in student achievement. For example, 49 hours of professional development in a school year boosts student achievement by 21 percent. "Sustained" is defined as between 30 to 100 hours a year.

Data Teams should provide the collaborative, sustained, intensive, continuous professional development described above, and it is imperative for leaders to establish the expectations and set the direction for this type of professional development (Reeves, 2009). Attendance at conferences, contracting with a consultant, and professional reading can be very effective methods to provide learning opportunities for teachers that may result in new learning for teachers. However, if those professional development activities don't result in changing instructional practice and in increased student achievement (Hattie, 2009), then these activites are not worth the investment of energy or resources. Professional development activites should strengthen instruction and therefore improve student learning.

The Data Teams structure provides job-embedded, continuous, team-based, collaborative, results-oriented, reflective, hands-on, practical, and sustainable professional development. It drives the instructional core because it impacts instructional practice and therefore student learning.

Strategies for Making Data Teams
Your Primary Form of Professional Development

Use the following approaches to make Data Teams your primary form of professional development:

1. Make the time for it. In Chapter 7 we talked about finding time for Data Teams. Many schools exchange the three to five days allotted for professional development at a site for time with Data Team meetings. With this strategy, the use of Data Teams becomes *the* professional development at the site.

2. Align the topics of your professional development with school-wide improvement goals and thus with Data Team goals (if these are aligned with the school). Topics may not align to the focus area of each team but may provide professional development on instructional strategies and formative assessment.

3. Differentiate professional development. The topic of professional development is designed to meet the specific needs of each team by using the instructional experts on each team (not always the Data Team leader) as the vehicle for "teaching the teachers." The professional development then becomes collaborative and "on the job" because it occurs within a Data Team meeting.

4. At the district level, align all professional development topics with the Data Teams process. This may include Data Teams training, working with Data Team leaders, working with administrators guiding the process, and providing formative assessment as examples.

While changing the way schools and districts approach professional development may seem like a daunting task, if the current methods are not resulting in improved instructional practices and increased student learning, then the approach needs to change. When schools and districts use Data Teams as professional development, learning occurs, and it becomes "just the way we do professional learning; just the way we do business as teachers."

ONE FINAL WORD:
SUSTAINING THE DATA TEAMS PROCESS

You sustain Data Teams by focusing on the right work. The right work is improving teaching and leadership—and thus improving learning for all students.

Schools may not believe that the use of Data Teams is an effective way to approach school improvement and therefore may not jump on the Data Teams bandwagon in the initial stages of implementation. However, when our teaching and leadership practices change as a result of using the Data Teams process, we see results in student learning. When we see results in student learning, we start believing that we are doing the right thing. Data Teams are action oriented, and teams will see an immediate impact as a result of their work.

As a leader in the Data Teams process, you can sustain this work by marrying effective collaboration with good use of data. You can impact teaching and learning by formalizing and structuring your Data Teams with specific processes and purposes. You can sustain this work by aligning the school improvement goals, professional development, and assessment in your schools and districts. And as a leader, you can sustain this process by monitoring and providing feedback to Data Teams. By making Data Teams your "one thing" and focusing your professional development on Data Teams, you will sustain the process. And lastly, by celebrating the results of your hard work and the impact of your work, you will sustain the process.

> *The final challenge—and the one that solidifies success—is to build so much momentum that change is unstoppable, that everything reinforces the new behavior, that even the resistors get on board—exactly the momentum that develops in winning streaks.*
>
> ROBERT MOSS KANTER

Data Teams Templates

STEP 1 TEMPLATE

Data Team:
Date of Meeting:
Assessment:

Teacher	# Students	# Proficient and Higher	% Proficient and Higher	# Close to Proficiency	% Close to Proficiency	Students Close to Proficiency	# Far to Go But Likely to Become Proficient	% Far to Go But Likely to Become Proficient	Students Far to Go But Likely to Become Proficient	# Intervention (Far to Go and Not Likely to Become Proficient)	% Intervention (Far to Go and Not Likely to Become Proficient)	Intervention Students (Far to Go and Not Likely to Become Proficient)
TEAM												

STEP 2 TEMPLATE

Identify strengths and performance errors. Please indicate one priority per student group.

Students Proficient or Higher	
Performance Strengths	**Inference**
Next Steps	**Inference**

Students Close to Proficient	
Performance Strengths	**Inference**
Performance Errors and Misconceptions	**Inference**

STEP 2 TEMPLATE *(continued)*

Students Far to Go

Performance Strengths	Inference

Performance Errors and Misconceptions	Inference

Intervention Students

Performance Strengths	Inference

Performance Errors and Misconceptions	Inference

STEP 3 TEMPLATE

SMART goal statement:

The percentage of _____ scoring proficient
                              [student group]

or higher in _____ will increase from
                              [content area]

_____ to _____ by the end of _____
[current reality percentage]   [goal percentage]   [month or quarter]

as measured by _____ administered on _____ .
                     [assessment tool]   [specific date]

STEP 4 TEMPLATE

Students Proficient or Higher

Prioritized Next Step:

Selected Instructional Strategy	Learning Environment	Time—Frequency and Duration	Materials for Teachers and Students	Assignments and Assessments— Where will students be required to use the strategy?

Students Close to Proficient

Prioritized Need:

Selected Instructional Strategy	Learning Environment	Time—Frequency and Duration	Materials for Teachers and Students	Assignments and Assessments— Where will students be required to use the strategy?

STEP 4 TEMPLATE *(continued)*

Students Far to Go

Prioritized Need:

Selected Instructional Strategy	Learning Environment	Time—Frequency and Duration	Materials for Teachers and Students	Assignments and Assessments— Where will students be required to use the strategy?

Intervention Students

Prioritized Need:

Selected Instructional Strategy	Learning Environment	Time—Frequency and Duration	Materials for Teachers and Students	Assignments and Assessments— Where will students be required to use the strategy?

STEP 5 TEMPLATE

Students Proficient or Higher

Prioritized Next Step:

Selected Instructional Strategy:

Results Indicators	Adult Behaviors:	
	Student Behaviors:	
	What to Look For in Student Work:	

Students Close to Proficient

Prioritized Need:

Selected Instructional Strategy:

Results Indicators	Adult Behaviors:	
	Student Behaviors:	
	What to Look For in Student Work	

STEP 5 TEMPLATE *(continued)*

Students Far to Go

Prioritized Need:

Selected Instructional Strategy:

Results Indicators	Adult Behaviors:	
	Student Behaviors:	
	What to Look For in Student Work:	

Intervention Students

Prioritized Need:

Selected Instructional Strategy:

Results Indicators	Adult Behaviors:	
	Student Behaviors:	
	What to Look For in Student Work	

References

Abrahamson, E. (2004). *Change without pain.* Boston, MA: Harvard Business School Press.

Ainsworth, L. (2003a). *Power standards.* Englewood, CO: Lead + Learn Press.

Ainsworth, L. (2003b). *"Unwrapping" the standards.* Englewood, CO: Lead + Learn Press.

Ainsworth, L., & Viegut, D. J. (2006). *Common formative assessments: How to connect standards-based instruction and assessment.* Thousand Oaks, CA: Corwin Press.

Ancona, D., Malone, T. W., Orlikowski, W. J., & Senge, P. M. (2007). In praise of the incomplete leader. *Harvard Business Review 12*(11), 92–100.

Anderson, K. (2010). *Data teams success stories, volume 1.* Englewood, CO: Lead + Learn Press.

Andrews, R., & Soder, R. (1987). Principal leadership and student achievement. *Educational Leadership 44*(6), 9–11.

Bamberg, M., & Andrews, M. (2004). *Considering counter narratives.* Amsterdam: Benjamins.

Bandura, A. (1997). *Self-efficacy: The exercise of control.* New York: W.H. Freeman & Company.

Barber, M. (2009). From system effectiveness to system improvement: Paradigms and relationships. In Hargreaves, A., & Fullan, M. (Eds.), *Change wars.* Bloomington, IN: Solution Tree Press.

Becker, H. S., & Geer, B. (1960). Latent culture. *Administrative Science Quarterly 5*, 303–313.

Bernhardt, V. (1998). *Data analysis for comprehensive schoolwide improvement.* Larchmont, NY: Eye on Education.

Bossidy, L., & Charan, R. (2002). *Execution: The discipline of getting things done.* New York: Crown Business.

Bottoms, G., & Fry, B. (2009). *That district leadership challenge: Empowering principals to improve teaching and learning.* Atlanta, GA: Southern Regional Educational Board (SREB).

Bryk, A. S., & Schneider, B. (2002). *Trust in schools: A core resource for improvement.* New York: Russell Sage.

Carter, G. R. (1997). *The American school superintendent: Leading in an age of pressure.* San Francisco: Jossey-Bass.

Chrispeels, J. H., Burke, P. H., Johnson, P., & Daly, A. J. (2008). Aligning mental models of district and school leadership teams for reform coherence. *Education and Urban Society 40*(6), 73.

Chrispeels, J. H., & Gonzales, M. (2009). The challenge of systemic change in complex educational systems. In Harris, A., & Chrispeels. J. H., *Improving schools and educational systems.* New York: Routledge.

City, E. A., Elmore, R. E., Fiarman, S. E., & Teitel, L. (2009). *Instructional rounds in education: A network approach to improving teaching and learning.* Cambridge, MA: Harvard Education Press.

Collins, J. (2001). *Good to great: Why some companies make the leap . . . and others don't.* New York: Harper Business.

Covey, S. (2004). *The 8th habit.* New York: Free Press.

Darling-Hammond, L. (2010). *The flat world and education: How America's commitment to equity will determine our future.* New York: Teacher College Press.

Darling-Hammond, L., Barron, B., Pearson, P. D., Schoenfeld, A. H., Stage, E. K., Zimmerman, T .D., & Tilson, J. L. (2008). *Powerful learning: What we know about teaching for understanding.* San Francisco: Jossey-Bass.

Darling-Hammond, L., & Bransford, J. (Eds.). (2005). *Preparing teachers for a changing world: What teachers should learn and be able to do.* San Francisco: Jossey-Bass.

Darling-Hammond, L., & Richardson, N. (2009). Teacher learning: What matters. *Educational Leadership 66*(5), 46–53.

Darling-Hammond, L., Wei, R. C., Andree, A., Richardson, N., & Orphanos, S. (2009). *Professional learning in the learning profession: A status report on teacher development in the U.S. and abroad.* Oxford, OH: NSDC.

DuFour, R., DuFour, R., & Eaker, R. (1998). *Professional learning communities at work.* Bloomington, IN: Solution Tree Press.

DuFour, R., DuFour, R., & Eaker, R. (2008). *Revisiting professional learning communities at work: New insights for improving schools.* Bloomington, IN: Solution Tree Press.

Duke, D. (2007). Turning schools around: What are we learning about the process, and those who do it? *Education Week 26*(24), 35–37.

Earl, L. M., & Katz, S. (2006). *Leading schools in a data-rich world.* Thousand Oaks, CA: Corwin Press.

Elmore, R. F. (2004). *School reform from the inside out: Policy, practice, and performance.* Cambridge, MA: Harvard Education Press.

Filbin, J. F. (2008). *Examining the effects of changes in pedagogical precision, principal data use, and student achievement on collective efficacy* (Unpublished dissertation). Denver, CO: University of Denver.

Fullan, M. (2006). *Turnaround leadership.* San Francisco: Jossey-Bass.

Fullan, M. (2008a). *The six secrets of change: What the best leaders do to help their organizations survive and thrive.* San Francisco: Jossey-Bass.

Fullan, M. (2008b). *What's worth fighting for in the principalship?* New York: Teacher College Press.

Fullan, M. (Ed.). (2009a). *The challenge of change: Start school improvement now.* 2nd ed. Thousand Oaks, CA: Corwin Press.

Fullan, M. (2009b). Have theory, will travel: A theory of action for system change. In Hargreaves, A., & Fullan, M. (Eds.), *Change wars.* Bloomington, IN: Solution Tree Press.

Fullan, M. (2010). *All systems go: The change imperative for whole system reform.* Thousand Oaks, CA: Corwin Press.

Gagne, R. (1985). *The conditions of learning and the theory of instruction.* 4th ed. New York: Holt, Rinehart & Winston.

Gallimore, R. R., Ermeling, B. A., Saunders, W. M., & Goldenberg, C. C. (2009). Moving the learning of teaching closer to practice: Teacher education implications of school-based inquiry teams. *The Elementary School Journal 109*(5), 537–553.

Garmston, R. J., & Wellman, B. M. (1999). *The adaptive school.* Norwood, MA: Christopher-Gordon Publishers.

Graham, M. W. (March 1997). School principals: Their roles and preparation. Paper presented at the National Conference on Creating Quality Schools, Oklahoma City, OK.

Guskey, T. R. (2005). *Benjamin S. Bloom: Portraits of an educator.* Lanham, MD: Rowman & Littlefield.

Hallinger, P., & Heck, R. (1996). Reassessing the principal's role in school effectiveness: A review of empirical research, 1980–1995. *Educational Administration Quarterly 32*(1), 5–44.

Hanushek, E. A. (January 2004). Some simple analytics of school quality. NBER Working Paper No. W10229. Cambridge, MA: National Bureau of Economic Research.

Hargreaves, A., & Fullan, M. (Eds.). (2009). *Change wars.* Bloomington, IN: Solution Tree Press.

Hargreaves, A., & Shirley, D. (2009). *The fourth way.* Thousand Oaks, CA: Corwin Press.

Harris, A., & Chrispeels, J. H. (2009). *Improving schools and educational systems: International perspectives.* New York: Routledge.

Hattie, J. (2009). *Visible learning: A synthesis of over 800 meta-analyses relating to achievement.* New York: Routledge.

Hattie, J. (2010). Personal communication, June 29, 2010.

Hayes-Jacobs, H. (Ed.). (2010). *Curriculum 21: Essential education for a changing world.* Alexandria, VA: ASCD.

Heck, R. H., Larsen, T. J., & Marcoulides, G. A. (1990). Instructional leadership and school achievement: Validation of a causal model. *Educational Administration Quarterly 26*(2), 94–125.

Heck, R. H., Marcoulides, G. A., & Lang, P. (1991). Principal instructional leadership and school achievement: The application of discriminant techniques. *School Effectiveness and School Improvement 2*(2), 115–135.

Hersey, P., & Blanchard, K. H. (1977). *Management of organizational behavior: Utilizing human resources.* 3rd ed. Upper Saddle River, NJ: Prentice Hall.

Higgins, M., Young, L., Weiner, J., & Wlodarczyk, S. (2010). Leading teams of leaders: What helps team member learning? *Phi Delta Kappan 91*(4), 41–45.

Honig, M. I., Copland, M. A., Rainey, L., Lorton, J. A., & Newton, M. (2010). Creating central office transformation for district-wide teaching and learning improvement. University of Washington, Center for the Study of Teaching and Policy.

Hord, S. M., & Sommers, W. A. (2008). *Leading professional learning communities: Voices from research and practice.* Thousand Oaks, CA: Corwin Press.

Jackson, D. (2009). The creation of knowledge networks: Collaborative inquiry for schools and system improvement. In Harris, A., & Chrispeels, J. H., *Improving schools and educational systems: International perspectives.* New York: Routledge.

Jacobson D. (2010). Coherent instructional improvement and PLCs: Is it possible to do both? *Phi Delta Kappan 91*(6), 38–45.

Jorgenson. O., & Peal, C. (2008). When principals lose touch with the classroom. *Principal 87*(4), 52–55.

Joyce, B., & Showers, B. (2002). *Student achievement through staff development.* 3rd ed. Alexandria, VA: ASCD.

Knight, J. (2009). What can we do about teacher resistance? *Phi Delta Kappan 90*(7), 508–513.

Kotter, J. P. (1996). *Leading change.* Cambridge, MA: Harvard Business School Press.

Leithwood, K., Day, C., Sammons, P., Harris, A., & Hopkins, D. (2007). *Seven strong claims about successful schools leadership.* Nottingham, England: National College of School Leadership.

Leithwood, K., & Jantzi, D. (2008). Linking leadership to student learning: The contributions of leader efficacy. *Educational Administration Quarterly 44*(4), 496.

Levin, B. (2008). *How to change 5000 schools: A practical and positive approach for leading change at every level.* Cambridge, MA: Harvard Education Press.

Levin, B. (2009). Reform without (much) rancor. In Hargreaves, A., & Fullan, M. (Eds.), *Change wars.* Bloomington, IN: Solution Tree Press.

Louis, K. S., Leithwood, K., Wahlstrom, K. L., & Anderson, S. E., (2010). *Learning from leadership: Investigating the links to improved student learning.* Center for Applied Research and Educational Improvement/University of Minnesota and Ontario Institute for Studies in Education/University of Toronto

Louis, M. R. (1980). Organizations as culture-bearing milieu. In Pondy, L. R., et al. (Eds.), *Organizational symbolism.* Greenwich, CT: JAI.

MacIver, M., & Farley-Ripple, E. (2008). Bringing the district back. In *The role of the central office in instruction and achievement.* Alexandria, VA: Educational Research Services.

Mangin, M. M. (2007). Facilitating elementary principals' support for instructional teacher leadership. *Educational Administration Quarterly 43*(3), 319.

Marks, H. M., & Printy, S. M. (2003). Principal leadership and school performance: An integration of transformational and instructional leadership. *Educational Administration Quarterly 39*(3), 370–397.

Marsh, J. A., Kerr, K. A., Ikemoto, G. S., Darilek, H., Suttorp, M., & Zimmer, R. W. (2005). *The role of districts in fostering instructional improvement: Lessons from three urban districts partnered with the Institute for Learning.* Santa Monica, CA: RAND.

Marzano, R. J. (2003). *What works in schools: Translating research into action.* Alexandria, VA: ASCD.

Marzano, R. J. (2007). *The art and science of teaching.* Alexandria, VA: ASCD.

Marzano, R. J. (2008). *Getting serious about school reform: Three critical commitments.* Denver, CO: Marzano and Associates.

Marzano, R. J. (2009). Setting the record straight on "high yield" strategies. *Phi Delta Kappan 91*(1), 30–37.

Marzano, R. J., Pickering, D., & Pollock, J. (2001). *Classroom instruction that works.* Alexandria, VA: ASCD.

Marzano, R. J., & Waters, T. (2009). *District leadership that works: Striking the right balance.* Bloomington, IN: Solution Tree Press.

Marzano, R. J., Waters, J. T., & McNulty, B. A. (2005). *School leadership that works: From research to results.* Alexandria, VA: ASCD.

Murphy, J., & Hallinger, P. (1988). In Elmore, R. (2004), *School reform from the inside out: Policy, practice, and performance.* Cambridge, MA: Harvard Education Press.

Murphy, J., & Meyers, C. V. (2008). *Turning around failing schools: Leadership lessons from the organizational sciences.* Thousand Oaks, CA: Corwin Press.

Newman, F. M., Marks, H. M., & Gamoran, A. Cited in Darling-Hammond, L. (2006), No child left behind and high school reform. *Harvard Educational Review 76*(4), 642–667. Cambridge, MA: Harvard Education Press.

Nye, B., Konstantopoulos, A., & Hedges, L. V. (2004). How large are teacher effects? *Educational Evaluation and Policy Analysis 26*(3), 237–257.

Pappano, L. (March/April 2007). More than "making nice": Getting teachers to (truly) collaborate. *Harvard Education Letter 23*(2). Cambridge, MA: Harvard Education Press.

Parsley, D., & Galvin, M. (2008). Think systemically, act systematically. *Journal of Scholarship and Practice 4*(4), 4–10.

Patterson, K., Grenny, J., Maxfield, D., McMillan, R., & Switzler, A. (2008). *Influencer: The power to change anything.* New York: McGraw-Hill.

Peery, A. (2009). *Writing matters in every classroom.* Englewood, CO: Lead + Learn Press.

Peters, T. (2003). *Re-imagine! Business excellence in a disruptive age.* London: Dorling Kindersley.

Pfeffer J., & Sutton, R. (2000). *The knowing-doing gap: How smart companies turn knowledge into action.* Boston: Harvard Business School Press.

Popham, W. J. (2009). *Unlearned lessons.* Cambridge, MA: Harvard Education Press.

Portin, B. S., Knapp, M. S., Dareff, S., Feldman, S., Russell, F., Samuelson, C., & Ling Yeh, T. (2009). *Leadership for learning improvement in urban schools.* Center for the Study of Teaching and Policy, University of Washington.

Reeves, D. B. (2002). *The leaders' guide to standards.* San Francisco, CA: Jossey-Bass.

Reeves, D. B. (2004). *Accountability for learning.* Alexandria, VA: ASCD.

Reeves, D. B. (2005). *Accountability in action.* 2nd ed. Englewood, CO: Lead + Learn Press.

Reeves, D. B. (2006). *The learning leader: How to focus school improvement for results.* Alexandria, VA: ASCD.

Reeves, D. B. (Ed.). (2007). *Ahead of the curve.* Bloomington, IN: Solution Tree Press.

Reeves, D. B. (2008). *Reframing teacher leadership to improve your school.* Alexandria, VA: ASCD.

Reeves, D. B. (2009). Level-five networks: Making significant change in complex organizations. In Hargreaves, A., & Fullan, M. (Eds.), *Change wars.* Bloomington, IN: Solution Tree Press.

Reeves, D. B. (2010). *Transforming professional development into student results.* Alexandria, VA: ASCD.

Robinson, V. M. J. (2007). *School leadership and student outcomes: Identifying what works and why.* Winmallee, Australia: Australian Council of Educational Leadership (ACEL), no. 41.

Robinson, V. M. J., Lloyd, C. A., & Rowe, K. J. (2008). The impact of leadership on student outcomes: An analysis of the differential effects of leadership types. *Educational Administration Quarterly 44*(5), 635–674.

Rogers, E. M. (1962). *Diffusion of innovations.* New York: Free Press.

Rogers, E. M. (2003). *Diffusion of innovations.* 5th ed. New York: Free Press.

Salmonowicz, M. (2009). Lessons from the intersection of research and practice: Seven recommendations for turning around low performing schools may help leaders facing this challenge. *Phi Delta Kappan 91*(3), 19–24.

Saunders, W. M., Goldenberg, C. N., & Gallimore, R. (2009). Increasing achievement by focusing on grade-level teams: A prospective, quasi-experimental study of title I schools. *American Educational Research Journal 44*(4), 1006–1033.

Schlechty, P. (2009). *Leading for learning.* San Francisco, CA: Jossey-Bass.

Schmoker, M. J. (1999). *Results: The key to continuous school improvement.* 2nd ed. Alexandria, VA: ASCD.

Schmoker, M. (2006). *Results now.* Alexandria, VA: ASCD.

Senge, P. (1990). *The fifth discipline.* New York: Random House.

Shepard, L., Hammerness, K., Darling-Hammond, L., Rust, F., Snoweden, J. B., Gordon, E., Gutierrez, C., et al. (2005). Assessment. In Darling-Hammond, L., & Bransford, J. (Eds.), *Preparing teachers for a changing world: What teachers should learn and be able to do.* San Francisco: Jossey-Bass.

Simmons, J. (2006). *Breaking through: Transforming urban schools.* Amsterdam, NY: Teacher College Press.

Smith, L. (2008). *Schools that change: Evidence-based improvement and effective change leadership.* Thousand Oaks, CA: Corwin Press.

Sparks, D. (2005). *Leading for results: Transforming teaching, learning, and relationships in schools.* Thousand Oaks, CA: Corwin Press.

Spillane, J. P. (2006). *Distributed leadership.* San Francisco: Jossey-Bass.

Stein, M. K., & Coburn, C. E. (2008). Architecture for learning: A comparative analysis of two urban school districts. *The American Journal of Education 114*(4), 583–626.

Stiggins, R. J., Arter, J. A., Chappuis, J., & Chappuis, S. (2004). *Classroom assessment for student learning.* Portland, OR: Assessment Training Institute.

Supovitz, J. A. (2006). *The case for district-based reform: Leading, building, and sustaining school improvement.* Cambridge, MA: Harvard Education Press.

Supovitz, J. A., & Christman, J. B. (2005). Small learning communities that actually learn: Lessons for school leaders. *Phi Delta Kappan 86*(9), 649–651.

Togneri W., & Anderson, S. E. (2003). *Beyond islands of excellence: What districts can do to improve instruction and achievement in all schools—A leadership brief* (Stock No. 303369). Washington, DC: Learning First Alliance.

Tschannen-Moran, M. (2004). *Trust matters: Leadership for successful schools.* San Francisco: Jossey-Bass.

Wade, R. K. (1985). *What makes a difference in in-service teacher education? A meta-analysis of the research.* (Ph.D. dissertation). University of Massachusetts.

Wahlstrom, K. L., & Louis, K. S. (2008). How teachers experience principal leadership: The roles of professional community, trust, efficacy, and shared responsibility. *Educational Administration Quarterly 44*(4), 458.

Weinbaum, E. H., & Supovitz, J. A. (2010). Planning ahead: Make program implementation more predictable. *Phi Delta Kappan 91*(7), 68–70.

White, S. H. (2005). *Beyond the numbers.* Englewood, CO: Lead + Learn Press.

White, S. H. (2009). *Leadership maps.* Englewood, CO: Lead + Learn Press.

Wiliam, D. (2007). Content then process: Teacher learning communities in the service of formative assessment. In Reeves, D. B. (Ed.), *Ahead of the curve.* Bloomington, IN: Solution Tree Press.

Willingham, D. T. (2009). Cited in Reeves, D. B. (2010). *Transforming professional development into student results.* Alexandria, VA: ASCD.

Zemelman, S., Daniels, H., & Hyde, A. (1998). *Best practice: New standards for teaching and learning in America's schools.* Portsmouth, NH: Heinemann.

Index